Armenian Mythology

Stories of Armenian Gods and Goddesses,
Heroes and Heroines, Hells & Heavens,
Folklore & Fairy Tales

Mardiros H. Ananikian

Armenian Mythology: Stories of Armenian Gods and Goddesses, Heroes and Heroines, Hells & Heavens, Folklore & Fairy Tales

For information and contact visit our website at:
IndoEuropeanPublishing.com

The present edition is a revised version of an earlier publication, produced in the current edition with completely new, easy to read format, and is set and proofread by Alfred Aghajanian for Indo-European Publishing.

Cover Design by Indo-European Design Team

ISBN: 978-1-60444-172-7

IndoEuropean
Publishing.com
Los Angeles, CA, USA

Contents

Author's Preface

THE ancient religion of Armenia was derived from three main sources: National, Iranian, and Asianic. The Asianic element, including the Semitic, does not seem to have extended beyond the objectionable but widely spread rites of a mother goddess. The National element came from Eastern Europe and must have had a common origin with the Iranian. But it, no doubt, represents an earlier stage of development than the Vedas and the Avesta. It is for the well-informed scholar of Indo-European religion to pronounce a judgement as to the value of the material brought together in this study. The lexical, folk-loristic, and literary heritage of the Armenians has much yet to disclose. No one can be more painfully conscious than the author of the defects of this work. He had to combine research with popular and connected exposition, a task far above his ability. The ancient material was not so scanty as broken. So analogy, wherever it could be found within the family, was called upon to restore the natural connections.

Among the numerous writers on Armenian mythology, three names stand high: Mgrdich Emin of Moscow, Prof. Heinrich Gelzer of Jena, and Father Leo Alishan of Venice. Emin laid the foundation of the scientific treatment of Armenian mythology in the middle of the nineteenth century, and his excellent contribution has become indispensable in this field. To Heinrich Gelzer, primarily a scholar of Byzantine history, we owe the latest modern study of the Armenian Pantheon. As for Alishan, he was a poet and an erudite, but had hardly any scientific training. So his *Ancient Faith of Armenia* is a naive production abounding in more or less inaccessible material of high value and in sometimes suggestive but more often strange

iv

speculations. Manug Abeghian will rightly claim the merit of having given to Armenian folklore a systematic form, while A. Aharonian's thesis on the same subject is not devoid of interest. Unfortunately Stackelberg's article, written in Russian, was accessible to the author only in an Armenian resume. Sandalgian's *Histoire Documentaire de l' Armenie*, which appeared in 1917 but came to the author's notice only recently, contains important chapters on ancient Armenian religion and mythology. The part that interprets Urartian inscriptions through ancient Greek and Armenian has not met with general recognition among scholars. But his treatment of the classic and medieval material is in substantial accord with this book. The main divergences have been noted.

Grateful thanks are due to the editors as well as the publishers for their forbearance with the author's idiosyncrasies and limitations. Also a hearty acknowledgement must be made here to my revered teacher and colleague Prof. Duncan B. Macdonald of the Hartford Theological Seminary, to Prof. Lewis Hodous of the Kennedy School of Missions, and to Dr. John W. Chapman of the Case Memorial Library for many fertile suggestions. Prof. Macdonald, himself an ardent and able folk-lorist, and Prof. Hodous, a student of Chinese religions, carefully read this work and made many helpful suggestions.

M. H. ANANIKIAN
Hartford, Connecticut,
April 23, 1922.

Introduction

The Political Background

LONG before the Armenians came to occupy the lofty plateau, south of the Caucasus, now known by their name, it had been the home of peoples about whom we possess only scanty information. It matters little for our present purpose, whether the older inhabitants consisted of different ethnic types, having many national names and lanuages, or whether they were a homogeneous race, speaking dialects of the same mother tongue and having some common name. For the sake of convenience we shall call them Urartians, as the Assyrians did. The Urartians formed a group of civilized states mostly centreing around the present city of Van. Although they left wonderful constructions and many cuneiform inscriptions, we depend largely on the Assyrian records for our information concerning their political history.

It would seem that the Urartians belonged to the same non-Aryan and non-Semitic stock of peoples as the so-called Hittites who held sway in the Western Asiatic peninsula long before Indo-European tribes such as Phrygians, Mysians, Lydians, and Bithynians came from Thrace, and Scythians and Cimmerians from the north of the Black Sea to claim the peninsula as their future home.

The Urartians were quite warlike and bravely held their own against the Assyrian ambitions until the seventh century B.C., when their country, weakened and disorganized through continual strife, fell an easy prey to the Armenian conquerors (640-600).

The coming of the Armenians into Asia Minor, according to the classical authorities, forms a part of the great exodus from Thrace. By more than one ancient and intelligent writer, they are declared to have been closely related to the Phrygians whom they resembled both in language and costume, and with whom they stood in Xerxes' army, according to Herodotus (1). Slowly moving along the southern shores of the Black Sea, they seem to have stopped for a while in what was known in antiquity as Armenia Minor, which, roughly speaking, lies southeast of Pontus and just northeast of Cappadocia. Thence they must have once more set out to conquer the promised land, the land of the Urartians, where they established themselves as a military aristocracy in the mountain fastnesses and the fortified cities, driving most of the older inhabitants northward, reducing the remainder to serfdom, taxing them heavily, employing them in their internal and external wars, and gradually but quite effectively imposing upon them their own name, language, religion, and cruder civilization. It is very natural that such a relation should culminate in a certain amount of fusion between the two races. This is what took place, but the slow process became complete only in the middle ages when the Turkish (Seljuk) conquest of the country created a terrible chaos in the social order.

Very soon after the Armenian conquest of Urartu, even before the new lords could organize and consolidate the land into anything like a monarchy, Armenia was conquered by Cyrus (558-529 B.C.), then by Darius (524-485 B.C.). After the meteoric sweep of Alexander the Great through the eastern sky, it passed into Macedonian hands. But in 190 B.C., under Antiochus the Great, two native satraps shook off the Seleucid yoke. One of them was Artaxias, who with the help of the fugitive Hannibal, planned and built Artaxata, on the Araxes, as his capital. Under the dynasty of this king, who became a legendary hero, the country prospered for a while and attained with Tigranes the Great (94-54 B.C.) an ephemeral greatness without precedent until then and without any parallel ever since. In 66 A.D. a branch of the Parthian (Arsacid) Dynasty was established in Armenia under the suzerainty and protection of Rome. The first king of this house was Tiridates I, formerly the head of the Magi of his country, who may have

2

done much in Armenia for the establishment of Zoroastrianism. It was under Tiridates II, a scion of this royal house, that, in the beginning of the fourth century of our era, Christianity, long present in the country, and often persecuted, achieved its fuller conquest.

Footnote

1. Herodotus, vii, 73. This view is confirmed by other evidence. The Armenian language, like Thracian, is a Satem language. The old Armenians were addicted to beer-drinking just like their Western brothers. The old Armenian ideal of human beauty was the large proportioned, bright (blue?) eyed, fair complexioned man. We shall later see that the Armenian religion also bears some important testimony to their original identity with the Thracians.

Chapter I

The Religious Development

THE URARTIANS believed in a supreme being, the god of heaven, whose name was Khaldi. If not the whole, at least a large part of the population called itself Khaldian, a name which survived the final downfall of the Urartian state in a province situated northwest of Armenia where evidently the old inhabitants were driven by the Armenian conquerors. In their ancient non-Aryan pantheon, alongside of Khaldi stood Theispas, a weather-god or thunderer of a very wide repute in Western Asia, and Artinis, the sun-god. These three male deities came to form a triad, under Babylonian influence. From the fact that in one Babylonian triad composed of Sin (the moon), Shamas (the sun) and Ramman (a weather-god), Sin is the lord of the heavens, scholars have concluded that Khaldi may have been also (or become) a moon-god.

Whether this be the case or not, the Urartian pantheon contains a secondary moon-god called Shelartish. Besides these no less than forty-six secondary, mostly local, deities are named in an official (sacrificial ?) list. The original Khaldian pantheon knew no female deity. Thus it stands in glaring contrast with Asianic (Anatolian) religions in which the mother goddess occupies a supreme position. But in the course of time, Ishtar of Babylon, with her singularly pervasive and migratory character, found her way into Urartu, under the name of Sharis (1).

One may safely assume that at least in the later stage of its political existence, long before the arrival of the Armenians on

4

the scene, Urartu had made some acquaintance with the Indo-Iranians and their Aryan manners and beliefs. For the Medes had begun their national career long before 935 B.C., and a little later the Scythians had established themselves in Manna, an Eastern dependency of Urartu (2).

As an undeniable evidence of such influences we may point to the fact that in Manna, Khaldi had become identified with Bag-Mashtu (Bag-Mazda) a sky-god and probably an older form of the Iranian Ahura Mazda.

It is in the midst of such a religion and civilization that the Armenians came to live. Their respect for it is attested by the fact that the ancient Urartian capital, Thuspa (the present Van), was spared, and that another (later) capital, Armavira in the North, became a sacred city for them, where according to the national legend even royal princes engaged in the art of divination through the rustling leaves of the sacred poplar (Armen.*Saus*). On the other hand the vestiges of Armenian paganism conclusively show that the newcomers lent to the Urartians infinitely more than they borrowed from them.

The Thracians and Phrygians, with whom the Armenians were related, had in later times a crude but mystic faith and a simple pantheon.

Ramsay, in his article on the Phrygians (3) assumes that the chief deity whom the Thracian influx brought into Asia Minor was male, and as the native religion was gradually adopted by the conquerors, this god associated himself with, and usurped certain functions of, the Asianic goddess. At all events the Phrygians, who had a sky-god called Bagos Papaios, must have had also an earth-goddess Semele (Persian Zamin) who no doubt became identified with some phase of the native goddess (Kybele, Ma, etc.). The confusion of the earth-goddess with the moon seems to have been a common phenomenon in the nearer East. Dionysos or Sabazios represented the principle of fertility of nature, without any marked reference to the human race. He was a god of moisture and vegetation. The corn that sustains life, and the wine and beer that gladden the heart, were his gifts. These things sprang from the bosom of mother earth,

5

through his mysterious influence, for the earth and he were lovers.

Further the Thracians and Phrygians at the winter solstice, held wild orgies (Bacchanalia), when naked women, wrought into frenzy by music and dance, and driven by priests, wandered in bands through fields and forests, shouting the name of the deity or a part of it (like Saboi), and by every barbarous means endeavouring to awaken the dead god into reproductive activity (4). He was imagined as passing rapidly through the stages of childhood, adolescence and youth. And as he was held to be incarnate in a bull, a buck, a man, or even in an infant, the festival reached its climax in the devouring of warm and bloody flesh just torn from a live bull, goat, or a priest. Sabazios under the name of Zagreus was thus being cut to pieces and consumed by his devotees. In this sacramental meal, the god no doubt became incarnate in his votaries and blessed the land with fertility (5).

We have no clear traces of such repulsive rites in what has been handed down to us from the old religion of the Armenians in spite of their proverbial piety. Whatever they have preserved seems to belong to another stratum of the Phrygo-Thracian faith (6).

A careful examination of this ancient material shows among the earliest Armenians a religious and mythological development parallel to that observed among other Indo-European peoples, especially the Satem branch of the race.

Their language contains an important fund of Indo-European religious words such as *Tiu* (Dyaus = Zeus = Tiwaz), "day-light," and *Di-kh* (pl. of*Di*, i.e. Deiva = Deus, etc.) , "the gods." When the ancient Armenians shouted, "Ti (or Tir), forward," they must have meant this ancient Dyaus Pitar who was also a war-god, and not *Tiur*, their much later very learned but peaceful scribe of the gods. Even the name of Varuna appears among them in the form of Vran (a cognate of Gr. *ouranos*) and in the sense of "tent," "covering." It is not impossible that *astwads*, their other word for "God," which in Christian times supplanted the heathen *Di-kh*, "Gods," was originally an epithet of the father of the gods and men, just like the *Istwo* of Teutonic mythology, of which it may well be a cognate (7).

The Perkunas of the Lithuanians and the Teutonic Fjorgynn, one as a god of heaven and of weather, and the other as a goddess of the earth, are still preserved in the Armenian words *erkin*, "heaven," and *erkir (erkinr?)* "earth" (8). The word and goddess, *iord, erd,* "earth," seems to survive in the Armenian *ard*, "land," "field."

Another ancient Armenian word for Mother-earth is probably to be found in *armat*, which now means "root." But in its adjectival form *armti-kh*, "cereals," it betrays a more original meaning which may shed some light upon the much disputed Vedic *aramati* and Avestic *armaiti*. The word *hoghm*, "wind," may have originally meant "sky," as cognate of *Himmel*. The Vedic and Avestic *vata* (Teut. *Votan?*) is represented in Armenian by *aud*, "air," "weather," "wind," while Vayu himself seems to be represented by more than one mythological name. Even the Vedic Aryaman and the Teutonic Irmin may probably be recognized in the name of Armenak, the better-known eponymous hero of the Armenians, who thus becomes identical with the ancient Dyaus-Tiwaz. To these may be added others whom we shall meet later. And in the Vahagn myths we see how, as in India and Teutonic lands, a violent storm-god has supplanted the grander figure of the heaven-god.

The oak (which in Europe was sacred to the sky-god) and water played an important part in the Armenian rites of the sacred fire. The sacred fire was, as in Europe, often extinguished in water. This religion was quite agricultural. In view of the general agreement of the Slavic and old Armenian data on this point, one may well ask whether the Thraco-Phrygian mysteries just described were not a localized development of the lightning worship so characteristic of the Slavic family to which the Thraco-Phrygians and the Armenians probably belonged (9). In fact, according to Tomaschek (10) the lightning-god had a very prominent place in the Thracian religion.

Lightning worship, more or less confused with the worship of a storm-god, was widely spread through Indo-European cults,

7

and it is attested in the Thracian family not only by the name of Hyagnis, a Phrygian satyr (see chapter on Vahagn) and Sbel Thiourdos, but also by the title of "Bull" that belonged to Dionysos and by such Greek myths as make him wield the lightning for a short time in the place of Zeus (11).

Soon after their coming into Urartu the Armenians fell under very strong Iranian influences, both in their social and their religious life. Now began that incessant flow of Iranian words into their language, a fact which tempted the philologists of a former generation to consider Armenian a branch of Iranian. When Xenophon met the Armenians on his famous retreat, Persian was understood by them, and they were sacrificing horses to the sun (or, perhaps to Mithra). But we find in the remnants of Armenian paganism no religious literature and no systematic theology, or cult of a purely Zoroastrian type. It would seem that the reformed faith of Iran penetrated Armenia very slowly and as a formless mass of popular beliefs which sometimes entered into mesalliances in their new home (12). In fact the names of the Zoroastrian gods and spirits found in Armenia bear a post-classic and pre-Sassanian stamp.

Finally the contact with Syria and with Hellenistic culture in Macedonian times and especially under Tigranes the Great (95-54 B.C.), brought into the religion of the country a new element. Statues of Syrian and Greek gods and goddesses were acquired in some way or other and set up in Armenian temples. Thus a small group of Semitic deities came into the Armenian pantheon, and interesting comparisons were established between the Armenian deities and the Olympians. Evidently under the influence of the Greek West and the Syrian South, the Armenians of the upper classes found the number of their gods inadequate and set themselves to create a pantheon of an impressive size. It was a time of conciliations, identifications, one might say of vandalistic syncretism that was tending to make of Armenian religion an outlandish motley. Their only excuse was that all their neighbours were following a similar course. It is, therefore, no wonder that the Sassanians during their short possession of Armenia in the middle of the third century seriously undertook to convert the land to the purer worship of the sacred fire. However, all was not lost in those days of syncretism and confusion. Most of the ancient traits can be easily recovered, while the tenacious conservatism of the common people saved a great amount of old and almost unadulterated material. This is, in short, both the historical development and the background of Armenian mythology. We should expect to find in it Urartian, Semitic, Armenian, Iranian, and Greek elements. But as a matter of fact the Urartian faith seems to have merged in the Armenian, while the Greek could only touch the surface of things, and the Semitic did not reach very far in its invasion. Therefore Armenian paganism, as it has come down to us, is mainly a conglomerate of native and Iranian elements.

Footnotes

1. It is barely possible that, as Jensen maintained in his *Hittiter und Armenier*, the Armenian word *shand*, "lightning," is a reminiscence of the Cicilian or Hittite *sanda, sandan* (see Frazer, GB I, part 4, *Adonis, Attis, and Osiris*, i.124 f.). Sanda, who was identified with Hercules, was a god of fertility, and may well have been a tribal variety of Tushup, the Hittite weather god.

2. We have now very clear evidence of the presence of Indo-Iranians among the Kassus of the lower part of the Zagros range, the Mittanis of Northern Mesopotamia, and the Hittites of Asia Minor, before and after the 15th century B.C.

3. ERE ix, 900.

4. American Indians had a similar rite according to Longfellow's *Hiawatha*, XIII. In the spring naked women rose on a certain night and walked around the fields, to make them fertile. The same thing is reported of some parts of Germany (Frazer, i. 138-139).

5. See L. R. Farnell, *The Cults of the Greek States*, Oxford, 1896-1909, vol. 5 ; artts. "Dionysos" and "Sabazios" in Roscher, Pauly-Wissowa, and Daremberg-Saglio; G. Davis, *The Asiatic Dionysus*, London, 1914.

6. The most unmistakable one of these is Hyagnis (see Chap. V and Appendix I). Hyas seems to be identical with Hayk, and Marsyas-Masses with the name of the sacred mountain Massis (Ararat). The Dio of Dionysus is often explained as "god," and may be found in the Armenian word *Di-kh*, "gods."

7. Codex La Cava calls *Istvo*, "Ostius," "Hostius." See A. V. Rydberg, *Teutonic Mythology*, tr. R. B. Anderson, London, 1889. As for *Astvads*, Agathangelos (5th cent.) defines it as "one who brings about," an explanation which seems to have struck the philosophical fancy of the ancient Armenian Fathers. Others have related it to *Hastvads*, "creature" or "creation," from the Persian *hast*, "exists." Another old writer saw in it the Cimmerian word for "unction." The Persian *yazd* the Avestic *astvat*, "incarnate," the Hindu Asdvada (Brahma?), the Celtic *Duez*, and the Teutonic *Tiwaz* (Ziu) (both of which are in reality cognates of the Greek Zeus), were drawn into the task of shedding light on the mysterious *Astvads*. Patrubani, a Hungarian Armenian who teaches in the University of Budapest, undertakes to explain it from the Vedic vashtu, "habitation," Gk. *astu*, "city," which by the addition of "ç" Indo-Germanic "ig" (to honor), would mean "that which the city worships." Prof. Marr of Moscow identifies *Astvads* with *Sabazios*, a view which the present writer held for a while independently of Marr.

8. The loss of an initial *p* before *r* or *l* is not an uncommon phenomenon in Armenian (see C. Brugmann and D. Delbriich, *Grundrt'ss der vergleichenden Grommatik der lndogerman. Sprachen*, Strassburg, 1886-1900, i. 503, and A. Meillet, *Grammaire armenienne*. The intervening *e* presents no difficulty. The Latin *periculum* is probably represented in Armenian by *erkiugh*, "fear."

9. The Slavic character of things Thraco~Phrygian has lately been attracting some attention (see G. Calderon, "Slavonic Elements in Greek Religion," *Classical Review* [1913]. The Letto-Slavic character of the Armenian language has been known for the last four decades through the researches of Hubschmann. Here it may be noted that something of this had already been observed in the folk-lore of the Armenians (see Chalatianz, *Intro.*).

10. *Die alten Thraker*, Vienna, 1893-4 (SW AW), ii. 60.

11. Gladys M. N. Davis, in a recent work called *The Asiatic Dionysos*, London, 1914, has revived an older theory that would identify Dionysos

with the Vedic *Soma*. This book has been very severely criticised, but its main contention is worthy of further investigation.

12. See also A. Meillet, "Sur les termes religieux iraniens en Armenien," in *Revue des etudes armeniennes*, i, fasc. 3, 1921; M. H. Ananikian, " Armenia," in ERE.

Chapter II

Chief Deities

STRABO, the celebrated Greek traveller of the first century of our era, in his notice of the Anahit worship at Erez (or Eriza), says that "both the Medes and the Armenians honour all things sacred to the Persians, but above everything Armenians honour Anahit."

An official (or priestly) reorganization of the national pantheon must have been attempted about the beginning of the Christian era. Agathangelos tells us plainly that King Khosrau, on his return from successful incursions into Sassanian lands, "commanded to seek the *seven* great altars of Armenia, and honoured (with all sorts of sacrifices and ritual pomp) the sanctuaries of his ancestors, the Arsacids." These sanctuaries were the principal temples of the seven chief deities whose names are: Aramazd, Anahit, Tiur, Mihr, Baal-Shamin (pronounced by the Armenians Barshamina), Nane, and Astghik. It is possible that these gods and goddesses were all patrons (genii) of the seven planets (1). If so, then Aramazd was probably the lord of Jupiter, Tiur corresponded to Mercury, Baal-Shamin or Mihr to the sun, Astghik to Venus, now called Arusyak, "the little bride." The moon may have been adjudged to Anahit or Nane (2). To these seven state deities, was soon added the worship of the very popular Vahagn, as the eighth, but he was in reality a native rival of Baal-Shamin and Mihr. We may add that there was a widely spread worship of the sun, moon, and stars as such, and perhaps a certain recognition of Spentaramet and Zatik. Armenia enjoyed also its full share of nature worship expressed in veneration for mountains, rivers, springs, trees, etc.

Of the main deities Aramazd was the most powerful and Anahit the most popular; with Vahagn they formed a triad. This preeminence of the three gods forced the rest of the pantheon into the less enviable position of secondary deities.

We know very little of the cultus of ancient Armenia, but we may perhaps say in general that it was not as much of a mixture as the pantheon.

We have two Armenian words for "temple," Mehyan, probably derived from Mithra-Mihr, and Tajar, which also meant a dining-hall. The plural of Bagin, "altar," also meant "temple" or "temples." Temples contained large treasures, and exercised hospitality towards all comers. Agathangelos (3) describes the sacrifices of Chosroes after his return from victorious incursions in these words:

He commanded to seek the seven great altars of Armenia, and he honoured the sanctuaries of his ancestors, the Arsacids, with white bullocks, white rams, white horses and mules, with gold and silver ornaments and gold embroidered and fringed silken coverings, with golden wreaths, silver sacrificial basins, desirable vases set with precious stones, splendid garments, and beautiful ornaments. Also he gave a fifth of his booty and great presents to the priests.
In Bayazid (the ancient Bagravand) an old Armenian relief was found with an altar upon which a strange animal stands, and on each side a man clothed in a long tunic. One is beardless, and carries a heavy club. The other has a beard. Their headgear, Phrygian in character, differs in detail. Both have their hands raised in the attitude of worship (4).

Probably the word for sacrifice was *spand* (Lithu. *sventa*, Persian *spenta* "holy," Gr. *spendô* "to pour a libation"); the place of sacrifice was called *Spandaran*, "the place of holy things"; and the priestly family that exercised supervision over the sacrificial rites was known as the Spandunis. They held a high rank among the Armenian nobility (5). Even to-day *Spandanotz* means "a slaughterhouse" and *Spananel,* "to slay." No other Armenian word has come down to us in the sense of "priest," seeing that *Kurm* is of Syriac or Asianic origin. Besides the Spandunis there were also the Vahunis attached to the temples of Vahagn, probably as priests. The Vahunis also were among the noble families.

The priesthood was held in such high esteem that Armenian kings often set up one or more of their sons as priests in celebrated temples. The burial place for priests of importance seems to have been Bagavan ("the town of the gods"). Whatever learning the country could boast was mainly in the possession of the sacerdotal classes.

Footnotes

1. Eghishe (5th cent.), speaking of the Sassanian Mihr, reports that the Persians considered him as the helper of "the seven gods," which means Auramazda with the six Amesha Spentas. Dolens and Khatch (pp. 201-203) maintain this view, and also aptly point to the Phoenician pantheon with seven Cabirs, and Eshmun the eighth. Even in India Aditi had seven, then with the addition of the sun, eight children.

2. Farther west, especially in Persianized Lydia, Anahita was represented with a crescent on her head.

3. Agathangelos, p. 34.

4. See detailed description in Saıdalgian's *Histoire documentaire,* p.794.

5. A thorough comparative study of the Armenian church rites is still a desideratum. When we have eliminated what is Byzantine or Syrian, we may safely assume that the rest is native and may have preserved bits of the pagan worship. Among these rites may be mentioned the abjuration of the devil in Lent, the Easter celebrations, the

Transfiguration roses and rose-water, the blessing of the grapes at the Assumption of the Virgin, the blessing of the four corners of the earth, etc.

Chapter III

Iranian Deities

1. Aramazd

WHOEVER was the chief deity of the Armenians when they conquered Urartu, in later times that important position was occupied by Aramazd. Aramazd is an Armenian corruption of the Auramazda of the old Persian inscriptions. His once widely spread cult is one of our strongest proofs that at least a crude and imperfect form of Zoroastrianism existed in Armenia. Yet this Armenian deity is by no means an exact duplicate of his Persian namesake. He possesses some attributes that remind us of an older sky-god.

Unlike the Ahura-Mazda of Zoroaster, he was supreme, without being exclusive. There were other gods beside him, come from everywhere and anywhere, of whom he was the father (1). Anahit, Nane and Mihr were regarded as his children in a peculiar sense (2). Although some fathers of the Greek Church in the fourth century were willing to consider Armenian paganism as a remarkable approach to Christian monotheism, it must be confessed that this was rather glory reflected from Zoroostrianism, and that the supremacy of Aramazd seems never to have risen in Armenia to a monotheism that could degrade other gods and goddesses into mere angels (Ameshas and Yazatas). Aramazd is represented as the creator of heaven and earth by Agathangelos in the same manner as by Xerxes who says in one of his inscriptions: "Auramazda is a great god, greater than all gods, who has created this heaven and this earth." The Armenian Aramazd was called "great" (3) and he must have been supreme in wisdom (Arm. *imastun,* a cognate of

16

mazdao) but he was most often characterised as *ari*, "manly," "brave," which is a good Armenian reminiscence of "Arya" (4).

He seems to have been of a benign and peaceloving disposition, like his people, for whom wisdom usually conveys the idea of an inoffensive goodness. As far as we know he never figures as a warlike god, nor is his antagonism against the principle of evil as marked as that of the Avestic Ahura Mazda. Nevertheless he no doubt stood and fought for the right (Armen. *ardar*, "righteous," Iran., *arda*, Sansk. *rita*).

Aramazd was above all the giver of prosperity and more especially of "abundance and fatness" in the land. Herein his ancient character of a sky-god comes into prominence. *Amenaber*, "bringer of all (good) things," was a beloved title of his (5). He made the fields fertile and the gardens and the vineyards fruitful, no doubt through rain. The idea of an Earth goddess had become dim in the Armenian mind. But it is extremely possible that in this connection, something like the Thracian or Phrygian belief in Dionysos lingered among the people in connection with Aramazd, for, besides his avowed interest in the fertility of the country, his name was sometimes used to translate that of the Greek Dionysos (6). Yet even the Persian Ahura-mazda had something to do with the plants (Ys. xliv. 4), and as Prof. Jackson says, he was a "generous" spirit.

It was in virtue of his being the source of all abundance that Aramazd presided at the *Navasard* (New Year's) festivals. These, according to the later (eleventh century) calendar, came towards the end of the summer and, beginning with the eleventh of August (Julian calendar), lasted six days, but originally the Armenian Navasard was, like its Persian prototype, celebrated in the early spring (7). In spite of the fact that al-Biruni, according to the later Persian (Semitic?) view, makes this a festival commemorating the creation of the world, one may be reasonably sure that both in Armenia and in Persia, it was an agricultural celebration connected with commemoration of the dead (see also chapter on Shahapet) and aiming at the increase of the rain and the harvests. In fact al-Biruni (9) informs us that in Navasard the Persians sowed "around a plate seven kinds of grain in seven columns and from

17

their growth they drew conclusions regarding the corn of that year" (9). Also they poured water upon themselves and others, a custom which still prevails among Armenians at the spring sowing and at the festival of the Transfiguration in June (10). This was originally an act of sympathetic magic to insure rain. Navasard's connection with Fravarti (Armen. *Hrotik*), the month consecrated to the ancestral souls in Persia and perhaps also in Armenia, is very significant, for these souls are in the old Aryan religion specially interested in the fertility of the land.

The later (Christian) Navasard in August found the second crop of wheat on the threshing floor or safely garnered, the trees laden with mellowing fruit and the vintage in progress (11). In many localities the Navasard took the character of a *fete champetre* celebrated near the sanctuaries, to which the country people flocked with their sacrifices and gifts, their rude music and rustic dances. But it was also observed in the towns and great cities where the more famous temples of Aramazd attracted great throngs of pilgrims. A special mention of this festival is made by Moses (II, 66) in connection with Bagavan, the town of the gods. Gregory Magistros (eleventh century) says that King Artaxias (190 B.C.) on his death-bed, longing for the smoke streaming upward from the chimneys and floating over the villages and towns on the New Year's morning, sighed :

"O! would that I might see the smoke of the chimneys,
And the morning of the New Year's day,
The running of the oxen and the coursing of the deer!
(Then) we blew the horn and beat the drum as it beseemeth Kings."

This fragment recalls the broken sentence with which al-Biruni's chapter on the Nauroz (Navasard) begins: "And he divided the cup among his companions and said, 'O that we had Nauroz every day!'" (12)

On these joyful days, Aramazd, the supremely generous and hospitable lord of Armenia, became more generous and hospitable (13). No doubt the flesh of sacrifices offered to him was freely distributed among the poor, and the wayworn traveller always found a ready welcome at the table of the

18

rejoicing pilgrims. The temples themselves must have been amply provided with rooms for the entertainment of strangers. It was really Aramazd-Dionysos that entertained them with his gifts of corn and wine.

Through the introduction of the Julian calendar the Armenians lost their Navasard celebrations. But they still preserve the memory of them, by consuming and distributing large quantities of dry fruit on the first of January, just as the Persians celebrated Nauroz, by distributing sugar (14). No information has reached us about the birth or parentage of the Armenian Aramazd. His name appears sometimes as Ormizd in its adjectival form. But we do not hear that he was in any way connected with the later Magian speculation about Auramazda, which (perhaps under Hellenistic influences) made him a son of the limitless time (Zervana Akarana) and a twin brother of Ahriman. Moreover, Aramazd was a bachelor god. No jealous Hera stood at his side as his wedded wife, to vex him with endless persecutions. Not even Spenta-Armaiti (the genius of the earth), or archangels, and angels, some of whom figure both as daughters and consorts of Ahura-mazda in the extant Avesta (Ys. 454 etc.), appear in such an intimate connection with this Armenian chief deity. Once only in a martyrological writing of the middle ages Anahit is called his wife (15). Yet this view finds no support in ancient authorities, though it is perfectly possible on *a priori* grounds.

Our uncertainty in this matter leaves us no alternative but to speculate vaguely as to how Aramazd brought about the existence of gods who are affiliated to him. Did he beget or create them? Here the chain of the myth is broken or left unfinished.

Aramazd must have had many sanctuaries in the country, for Armenian paganism was not the templeless religion which Magian Zoroastrianism attempted to become. The most highly honored of these was in Ani, a fortified and sacred city (perhaps the capital of the early Armenians) in the district of Daranali, near the present Erzinjan. It contained the tombs and mausolea of the Armenian kings (16) who, as Gelzer suggests, slept under the peaceful shadow of the deity. Here stood in later times a

Greek statue of Zeus, brought from the West with other famous images (17). It was served by a large number of priests some of whom were of royal descent (18). This sanctuary and famous statue were destroyed by Gregory the Illuminator during his campaign against the pagan temples.

Another temple or altar of Aramazd was found in Bagavan (town of the gods) in the district of Bagrevand (19), and still another on Mount Palat or Pashat along with the temple of Astghik. Moses of Khoren incidentally remarks (20) that there are four kinds of Aramazd, one of which is *Kund* (" bald") (21) Aramazd. These could not have been four distinct deities, but rather four local conceptions of the same deity, represented by characteristic statues (22).

2. Anahit

After Aramazd, Anahit was the most important deity of Armenia. In the pantheon she stood immediately next to the father of the gods, but in the heart of the people she was supreme. She was "the glory," "the great queen or lady," "the one born of gold," "the golden-mother."

Anahit is the Ardvi Sura Anahita of the Avesta, whose name, if at all Iranian, would mean "moist, mighty, undefiled," a puzzling but not altogether unbefitting appellation for the *yazata* of the earth-born springs and rivers. But there is a marked and well-justified tendency to consider the Persian Anahita herself an importation from Babylonia. She is thought to be Ishtar under the name of Anatu or the Elamite "Nahunta." If so, then whatever her popular character may have been, she could not find a place in the Avesta without being divested of her objectionable traits or predilections. And this is really what happened. But even in the Avestic portraiture of her it is easy to distinguish the original. This Zoroastrian golden goddess of the springs and rivers with the high, pomegranate-like breasts had a special relation to the fecundity of the human race. She was interested in child-birth and nurture, like Ishtar, under whose protection children were placed with incantation and solemn

20

rites. Persian maids prayed to her for brave and robust husbands. Wherever she went with the Persian armies and culture in Western Asia, Armenia, Pontus, Cappadocia, Phrygia, etc., her sovereignty over springs and rivers was disregarded and she was at once identified with some goddess of love and motherhood, usually with Ma or the Mater Magna. It would, therefore, be very reasonable to suppose that there was a popular Anahita in Persia itself, who was nothing less than Ishtar as we know her. This is further confirmed by the fact that to this day the planet Venus is called Nahid by the Persians (23).

The Armenian Anahit is also Asianic in character. She does not seem to be stepping out of the pages of the Avesta as a pure and idealized figure, but rather she came there from the heart of the common people of Persia, or Parthia, and must have found some native goddess whose attributes and ancient sanctuaries she assimilated. She has hardly anything to do with springs and rivers. She is simply a woman, the fair daughter of Aramazd, a sister of the Persian Mihr and of the cosmopolitan Nane. As in the Anahit Yashts of the Avesta, so also in Armenia, "golden" is her fairest epithet. She was often called "born in gold" or "the golden mother" probably because usually her statue was of solid gold. In the light of what has just been said we are not surprised to find that this goddess exhibited two distinct types of womanhood in Armenia, according to our extant sources. Most of the early Christian writers, specially Agathangelos, who would have eagerly seized upon anything derogatory to her good name, report nothing about her depraved tastes or unchaste rites.

If not as a bit of subtle sarcasm, then at least as an echo of the old pagan language, King Tiridates is made to call her "the mother of all sobriety," i.e. orderliness, as over against a lewd and ribald mode of life (24). The whole expression may also be taken as meaning "the sober, chaste mother." No suggestion of impure rites is to be found in Agathangelos or Moses in connection with her cultus.

On the other hand no less an authority than the geographer Strabo (63 B.C.-25A.D.) reports that the great sanctuary of

Anahit at Erez (or Eriza), in Akilisene (a district called also Anahitian (25) owing to the widely spread fame of this temple) was the centre of an obscene form of worship. Here there were hierodules of both sexes, and what is more, here daughters of the noble families gave themselves up to prostitution for a considerable time, before they were married. Nor was this an obstacle to their being afterwards sought in marriage (26).

Strabo is not alone in representing Anahit in this particularly sad light. She was identified with the Ephesian Artemis by the Armenians themselves. Faustus of Byzantium, writing in the fifth century, says of the imperfectly Christianized Armenians of the preceding century, that they continued "in secret the worship of the old deities in the form of fornication " (27). The reference is most probably to the rites of the more popular Anahit rather than her southern rival, Astghik, whom the learned identified with Aphrodite, and about whose worship no unchastity is mentioned. Medieval authors of Armenia also assert similar things about Anahit. Vanakan Vardapet says, "Astarte is the shame of the Sidonians, which the Chaldeans (Syrians or Mesopotamians) called Kaukabhta, the Greeks, Aphrodite, and the Armenians, Anahit" (28).

In a letter to Sahag Ardsruni, ascribed to Moses of Khoren (29), we read that in the district of Antzevatz there was a famous Stone of the Blacksmiths. Here stood a statue of Anahit and here the blacksmiths (no doubt invisible ones) made a dreadful din with their hammers and anvils. The devils (i.e. idols) dispensed out of a melting pot bundles of false medicine which served the fulfilling of evil desires, "like the bundle of St. Cyprian intended for the destruction of the Virgin Justina " (30). This place was changed later into a sanctuary of the Holy Virgin and a convent for nuns, called Hogeatz Vank.

There can be no doubt, therefore, that the Armenian Anahit admitted of the orgiastic worship that in the ancient orient characterized the gods and especially the goddesses of fertility. No doubt these obscene practices were supposed to secure her favor. On the other hand it is quite possible that she played in married life the well-known role of a mother of sobriety like Hera or rather Ishtar (31), the veiled bride and protector of wedlock, jealously watching over the love and faith plighted between husband and wife, and blessing their union. We may therefore interpret in this sense the above mentioned description of this goddess, which Agathangelos (32) puts in the mouth of King Tiridates: "The great lady (or queen) Anahit, who is the glory and lifegiver of our nation, whom all kings honour, especially the King of the Greeks (sic!), who is the mother of all sobriety, and a benefactress (through many favours, but especially through the granting of children) of all mankind; through whom Armenia lives and maintains her life." Although clear-cut distinctions and schematic arrangements are not safe in such instances, one may say in general that Aramazd once created nature and man, but he now (speaking from the standpoint of a speculative Armenian pagan of the first century) sustains life by giving in abundance the corn and the wine. Anahit, who also may have some interest in the growth of vegetation, gives more especially young ones to animals and children to man, whom she maternally tends in their early age as well as in their strong manhood. Aramazd is the god of the fertility of the earth, Anahit the goddess of the fecundity of the nation.

However, as she was deeply human, the birth and care of children could not be her sole concern. As a merciful and mighty mother she was sought in cases of severe illness and perhaps in other kinds of distress. Agathangelos mentions the care with which she tends the people. In Moses (33) we find that King Artaxias, in his last sickness, sent a nobleman to Erez to propitiate the tender-hearted goddess. But unlike Ishtar and the Persian Anahita, the Armenian Anahit shows no war-like propensities, nor is her name associated with death.

Like Aramazd, she had many temples in Armenia, but the most noted ones were those of Erez, Artaxata, Ashtishat, and Armavir (34). There was also in Sophene a mountain called the Throne of Anahit (35), and a statue of Anahit at the stone of the Blacksmiths. The temple at Erez was undoubtedly the richest sanctuary in the country and a favorite centre of pilgrimage. It was taken and razed to the ground by Gregory the Illuminator (36). It was for the safety of its treasures that the natives feared when Lucullus entered the Anahitian province (37).

23

Anahit had two annual festivals, one of which was held, according to Alishan, on the 15th of Navasard, very soon after the New Year's celebration. Also the nineteenth day of every month was consecrated to her. A regular pilgrimage to her temple required the sacrifice of a heifer, a visit to the river Lykos near-by, and a feast, after which the statue of the goddess was crowned with wreaths (38). Lucullus saw herds of heifers of the goddess (39), with her mark, which was a torch, wander up and down grazing on the meadows near the Euphrates, without being disturbed by anyone. The Anahit of the countries west of Armenia bore a crescent on her head.

We have already seen that the statues representing Anahit in the main sanctuaries, namely in Erez, Ashtishat, and probably also in Artaxata, were solid gold. According to Pliny (40) who describes the one at Erez, this was an unprecedented thing in antiquity. Not under Lucullus, but under Antonius did the Roman soldiers plunder this famous statue. A Bononian veteran who was once entertaining Augustus in a sumptuous style, declared that the Emperor was dining off the leg of the goddess and that he had been the first assailant of the famous statue, a sacrilege which he had committed with impunity in spite of the rumours to the contrary (41). This statue may have been identical with the (Ephesian) Artemis which, according to Moses, was brought to Erez from the west.

3. Tiur (Tir)

Outside of Artaxata, the ancient capital of Armenia (on the Araxes), and close upon the road to Valarshapat (the winter capital), was the best known temple of Tiur. The place was called Erazamuyn (Greek *oueironsos*), which probably means "interpreter of dreams" (43). Tiur had also another temple in the sacred city of Armavir (44).

He was no less a personage than the scribe of Aramazd, which may mean that in the lofty abode of the gods, he kept record of the good and evil deeds of men for a future day of reckoning, or what is more probable on comparative grounds, he had charge of writing down the decrees (*hraman*, Pers. *firman*) that were issued by Aramazd concerning the events of each human life (45). These decrees were no doubt recorded not only on heavenly tablets but also on the forehead of every child of man that was born. The latter were commonly called the "writ on the forehead" (46) which, according to present folklore, human eyes can descry but no one is able to decipher.

Besides these general and pre-natal decrees, the Armenians seem to have believed in an annual rendering of decrees, resembling the assembly of the Babylonian gods on the world-mountain during the Zagmuk (New Year) festival. They located this event on a spring night. As a witness of this we have only a universally observed practice.

In Christian Armenia that night came to be associated with Ascension Day. The people are surely reiterating an ancient tradition when they tell us that at an unknown and mystic hour of the night which precedes Ascension silence envelops all nature. Heaven comes nearer. All the springs and streams cease to flow. Then the flowers and shrubs, the hills and stones, begin to salute and address one another, and each one declares its specific virtue. The King Serpent who lives in his own tail learns that night the language of the flowers. If anyone is aware of that hour, he can change everything into gold by dipping it into water and expressing his wish in the name of God. Some report also that the springs and rivers flow with gold, which can be secured only at the right moment. On Ascension Day the people try to find out what kind of luck is awaiting them during the year, by means of books that tell fortune, or objects deposited on the previous day in a basin of water along with herbs and flowers. A veil covers these things which have been exposed to the gaze of the stars during the mystic night, and a young virgin draws them out one by one while verses divining the future are being recited (47). Whether Tiur originally concerned himself with all these things or not, he was the scribe of Aramazd. Being learned and skilful, he patronized and imparted both learning and skill. His temple, called the archive (48) of the scribe of Aramazd, was also a temple of learning and skill, i.e. not only a special sanctuary where one might pray for these things and make vows, but also a school where they were to be taught. Whatever else this vaunted learning and skill included, it must have had a special reference to the art of divination. It was a kind of Delphic oracle. This is indirectly attested by the fact that Tiur, who had nothing to do with light, was identified with Apollo in Hellenic times (49), as well as by the great fame for interpretation of dreams which Tiur's temple enjoyed. Here it was that the people and the grandees of the nation came to seek guidance in their undertakings and to submit their dreams for interpretation. The interpretation of dreams had long become a systematic science, which was handed down by a clan of priests or soothsayers to their pupils. Tiur must have also been the patron of such arts as writing and eloquence, for on the margin of some old Armenian MSS. of the book of Acts (chap. xiv, v. 12), the name of Hermes, for whom Paul was once mistaken because of his eloquence, was explained as "the god Tiur".

Besides all these it is more than probable that Tiur was the god who conducted the souls of the dead into the nether world. The very common Armenian imprecation, "May the writer carry him!" (50) or "The writer for him!" as well as Tiur's close resemblance to the Babylonian Nabu in many other respects, goes far to confirm this view.

In spite of his being identified with Apollo and Hermes, Tiur stands closer to the Babylonian Nabu (51) than to either of these Greek deities. In fact, Hermes himself must have developed on the pattern of Nabu. The latter was a god of learning and of wisdom, and taught the art of writing. He knew—and so he could impart—the meaning of oracles and incantations. He inspired (and probably interpreted) dreams. In Babylonia Nabu was identified with the planet Mercury.

But the name of Tiur is a proof that the Babylonian Nabu did not come directly from the South. By what devious way did he then penetrate Armenia?

The answer is simple. In spite of the puzzling silence of the Avesta on this point, Iran knew a god by the name of Tir. One of the Persian months, as the old Cappadocian and Armenian calendars attest, was consecrated to this deity (perhaps also the thirteenth day of each month). We find among the Iranians as well as among the Armenians, a host of theophorous names composed with "Tir" such as Tiribazes, Tiridates, Tiran, Tirikes, Tirotz, Tirith, etc., bearing unimpeachable witness to the god's popularity. Tiro-naKathwa is found even in the Avesta (52) as the name of a holy man. It is from Iran that Tir migrated in the wake of the Persian armies and civilization to Armenia, Cappadocia, and Scythia, where we find also Tir's name as Teiro on Indo-Scythian coins of the first century of our era (53).

We have very good reasons to maintain that the description of the Armenian Tiur fits also the Iranian Tir, and that they both were identical with Nabu. As Nabu in Babylonia, so also Tir in Iran was the genius presiding over the planet Mercury and bore the title of *Dabir*, "writer" (54).

But a more direct testimony can be cited bearing on the original identity of the Persian Tir with Nabu. The Neo-Babylonian king Nebuchadnezzar was greatly devoted to Nabu, his patron god. He built at the mouth of the Euphrates a city which he dedicated to him and called by a name containing the deity's name, as a component part. This name was rendered in Greek by Berossus (or Abydenus?) as *Teredon* and *Diridotis*, "given to Mercury." The latter form, says Rawlinson, occurs as early as the time of Alexander (55). The arrow-like writing-wedge was the commonest symbol of Nabu, and could easily give rise to the Persian designation (56). That the arrow seems to have been the underlying idea of the Persian conception of Nabu is better attested by the fact that both Herodotus and Armenian history know the older form of Tiran, Tigranes, as a common name. Tigranes is, no doubt, derived from Tigris, old Persian for "arrow."

4. Mihr (Mithra)

Our knowledge of the Armenian Mihr is unfortunately very fragmentary. He was unquestionably Iranian. Although popular at one time, he seems to have lost some ground when we meet with him. His name Mihr (Parthian or Sassanian for Mithra)

27

shows that he was a late comer. Nevertheless he was called the son of Aramazd, and was therefore a brother of Anahit and Nane. In the popular Zoroastrianism of Persia, especially in Sassanian times, we find that the sun (Mihr) and moon were children of Ormazd, the first from his own mother, or even from a human wife, and the moon, from his own sister (57). Originally Mihr may have formed in Armenia a triad with Aramazd and Anahit like that of Artaxerxes Mnemon's inscriptions. If so he soon had to yield that place to the national god Vahagn.

The Armenian Mithra presents a puzzle. If he was a genius of light and air, a god of war and contracts, a creature of Aramazd equal in might to his creator, as we find him to be in the Avesta, no trace of such attributes is left. But for the Armenians he was the genius or god of fire, and that is why he was identified with Hephaistos in syncretistic times (58). This strange development is perhaps further confirmed by the curious fact that until this day, the main fire festival of the Armenians comes in February, the month that once corresponded to the Mehekan (dedicated to Mihr) of the Armenian calendar. But it must not be overlooked that all over the Indo-European world February was one of the months in which the New Fires were kindled.

The connection of Mihr with fire in Armenia may be explained as the result of an early identification with the native Vahagn, who, as we shall see, was a sun, lightning, and fire-god. This conjecture acquires more plausibility when we remember that Mihr did not make much headway in Armenia and that finally Vahagn occupied in the triad the place which, by right and tradition, belonged to Mihr.

Of Mithraic mysteries in Armenia we hear nothing. There were many theophorous names compounded with his name, such as Mihran, Mihrdat. The Armenian word "Mehyan," "temple," seems also to be derived from his name.

We know that at the Mithrakana festivals when it was the privilege of the Great King of Persia to become drunk (with haoma?), a thousand horses were sent to him by his Armenian vassal. We find in the region of Sassun (ancient Tarauntis) a

28

legendary hero, called Meher, who gathers around himself a good many folk-tales and becomes involved even in eschatological legends. He still lives with his horse as a captive in a cave called Zympzymps which can be entered in the Ascension night. There he turns the wheel of fortune, and thence he will appear at the end of the world.

The most important temple dedicated to Mihr was in the village of Bagayarij (the town of the gods) in Derjan, Upper Armenia, where great treasures were kept. This sanctuary also was despoiled and destroyed by Gregory the Illuminator. It is reported that in that locality Mihr required human sacrifices, and about these Agathangelos also darkly hints (59). This is, however, very difficult to explain, for in Armenia offerings of men appear only in connection with dragon (i.e. devil) worship. On the basis of the association of Mihr with eschatological events, we may conjecture that the Armenian Mihr had gradually developed two aspects, one being that which we have described above, and the other having some mysterious relation to the under-world powers (60).

5. Spantaramet

The Amesha Spenta, Spenta Armaiti (holy genius of the earth) and the keeper of vineyards, was also known to the translators of the Armenian Bible who used her name in 2 Macc. vi. 7, to render the name of Dionysos. However, it would seem that she did not hold a place in the Armenian pantheon, and was known only as a Persian goddess. We hear of no worship of Spantaramet among the Armenians and her name does not occur in any passage on Armenian religion. It is very strange, indeed, that the translators should have used the name of an Iranian goddess to render that of a Greek god. Yet the point of contact is clear. Among the Persians Spenta Armaiti was popularly known also as the keeper of vineyards, and Dionysos was the god of the vine. But, whether it is because of the evident dissimilarity of sex or because the Armenians were not sufficiently familiar with Spantaramet, the translators soon (2 Macc. xiv. 33; 3 Macc. ii. 29) discard her name and use for

Dionysos "Ormzdakan god," i.e. Aramazd, whose peculiar interest in vegetation we have already noticed. Spenta Armaiti was better known to the ancient religion of Armenia as Santaramet, the goddess of the under-world.

The worship of the earth is known to Eznik (61) as a magian and heathen practice, but he does not directly connect it with the Armenians, although there can be little doubt that they once had an earth-goddess, called Erkir (Perkunas) or Armat, in their pantheon.

Footnotes

1. Agathangelos, p. 590.

2. Seeing that Anahit was in later times identified with Artemis and Nane, with Athene and Mihr and with Hephaistos, one may well ask whether this fathering of Aramazd upon them was not a bit of Hellenizing. Yet the Avesta does not leave us without a parallel in this matter.

3. Agathangelos, pp. 52, 61.

4. *Ibid.*, pp. 52, 61, 106.

5. *Ibid.*, p. 623.

6. It is noteworthy that his Christian successor is a hurler of the lightning.

7. See artts. "Calendar (Armenian)" and "Calendar (Persian)" in ERE iii. 70 f., 128 f.

8. Al-Biruni, *Chron.*, pp. 202-203.

9. This is an important instance of the Adonis gardens in the East,

overlooked by Frazer. Readers of his *Adonis, Attis, and Osiris* know how widely the custom had spread in the west.

10. See Chap. 8.

11. Gregory the Illuminator substituted the festival of St. John Baptist for that of the Navasard, but as that festival did not attain more than a local popularity (in Tarauntis) the later Fathers seem to have united it with the great festival of the Assumption of the Virgin, at which the blessing of the grapes takes place. These Christian associations gradually cost the old festival many of its original traits.

12. Al-Biruni, *Chron.*, p. 199.

13. Moses, ii. 66; Agathangelos, p. 623. Gelzer and others have made of his title of Vanatur, " hospitable," a separate deity. However corrupt the text of Agathangelos may be, i~ certainly does not justify this inference. Further, Vanatur is used in the Book of Maccabees to translate 1ieus Xenios.. For .a ,wller .discussion of this subject see art. " ArmenIa (Zoroastrian) "In ERE I. 795.

14. Al-Biruni, *Chron.*, p. 200.

15. Quoted by Alishan, p. 260. It is perhaps on this basis that Gelzer gives her the title of "mother of gods." This title finds no support in ancient records.

16. Agathangelos, p. 590. This cannot be Zoroastrian.

17. Moses, ii. 12.

18. *Ibid.*, ii. 53.

19. Agathangelos, p. 612.

20. Moses, i. 31.

21. *Kund* in Persian may mean "brave." But the word does not occur in Armenian in this sense.

22. The Iberians also had a chief deity called Armazi (a corruption of

Aramazd), whose statue, described as "the thunderer" or "a hurler of lightning," was set up outside of their capital, Mdskhit. A mighty river flowed between the temple and the city. As the statue was visible from all parts of the city, in the morning everyone stood on his house-roof to worship it. But those who wished to sacrifice, had to cross the river in order to do so at the temple. (Alishan, p. 314)

23. Whenever she may have come to Persia, her patronage over the rivers and springs need not be regarded as a purely Iranian addition to her attributes. The original Ishtar is a water goddess, and therefore a goddesss of vegetation, as well as a goddess of love and maternity. Water and vegetation underlie and symbolize all life whether animal or human. cf. *Mythology of all Races*, Boston, 1917, vi. 278 f.

24. Agathangelos, p. 52.

25. Dio. Cass., 36, 48; Pliny, HN v. 83.

26. Strabo, xi. 532C. Cumont thinks that this was a modification of ancient exogamy (see art. "Anahita " in ERE i. 414, and his *Les religions orientales dans le paganisme romain*, Paris, 1907, p. 287). Yet it is difficult to see wherein this sacred prostitution differs from the usual worship paid to Ishtar and Ma. As Ramsay explains it in his art. "Phrygians " (ERE ix. 900 f.) this is an act which is supposed to have a magical influence on the fertility of the land and perhaps also on the fecundity of these young women. Cf. artts. "Ashtart" (ERE ii. 115f.) and "Hierodouloi (Semitic and Egyptian)" (ERE vi. 672 f.).

27. Faustus, iii. 13.

28. Alishan, p. 263.

29. Moses, p. 294.

30. Justina was a Christian virgin of Antioch whom a certain magician called Cyprian tried to corrupt by magical arts, first in favor of a friend, then for himself. His utter failure led to his conversion, and both he and Justina were martyred together.

31. We have already seen (p. 11) that Ishtar as Sharis had secured a place in the Urartian pantheon.

32. Agathangelos, pp. 51, 61.

33. Moses, ii. 60.

34. *Ibid*, ii. 12.

35. Faustus, v. 25.

36. Agathangelos, p. 591.

37. Cicero, *De imperio Pompaeii*, p. 23.

38. Agathangelos, p. 59; Weber, p. 31.

39. Farther west Anahit required bulls, and was called Taurobolos.

40. HN xxxiii. 4; see Gelzer, p. 46.

41. Pliny, *loc. cit.*

42. Moses, ii. 16.

43. *Eraz*, "dream," is identical with the Persian word *raz*, "secret," ("occult," and perhaps also with the Slavic *raj*, "the other world," or "paradise." *Muyn* is now unintelligible and the *monsos* of the Greek is evidently a mere reproduction of the cryptic *muyn*.

44. Moses, ii. 12.

45. Tiur's name occurs also as Tre in the list of the Armenian months. In compound names and words it assumes the Persian form of Tir. We find a "Ti" in the old exclamation "(By) Ti or Tir, forward!" and it may be also in such compound forms as Ti-air, Ti-mann, a "lord," and Ti-kin, "a Ti-woman," i.e., "lady," "queen." Ti-air may be compared with Ti-rair, a proper name of uncertain derivation. However, owing to the absence of the "r" in Ti, one may well connect it with the older Tiv, a cognate of Indo-European Dyaus, Zeus, Tiwaz, etc., or one may consider it as a dialectical variety of the Armenian *di*, "god."

46. Eznik, pp. 150, 153, etc. Synonymous or parallel with this, we find also the word *bakht*, "fortuna."

47. Pshrank, p. 27 1. See for a fuller account Abeghian, p. 61 f .

48. Perhaps because, like the temple of Nabu in Borsippa, it contained a place symbolizing the heavenly archive in which the divine decrees were deposited.

49. Agathangelos.

50. "The Writer" was confused with the angel of death in Christian times. He is now called "the little brother of death." It is curious to note that the Teutonic Wotan, usually identified with Mercury, was also the conductor of souls to Hades.

51. Nabu, the city-god of Borsippa, once had precedence over Marduk himself in the Babylonian Pantheon. But when Marduk, the city god of Babylon, rose in importance with the political rise of his city, Nabu became the scribe of the gods and their messenger, as well as the patron of the priests. On the Babylonian New Year's Day (in the spring) he wrote on tablets, the destiny of men, when this was decided on the world mountain.

52. *Farvardin Yasht*, xxvii. 126.

53. Moulton, p. 435. Even the Arabs knew this deity under the name of 'Utarid, which also means Mercury, and has the epithet of "writer."

54. There lies before us no witness to the fact that the Armenians ever called the planet Mercury, Tiur, but it is probable. The Persians themselves say that Mercury was called Tir, "arrow," on account of its swiftness.

55. See G. Rawlinson's *Herodotus*, app. Bk. i, under Nebo.

56. Jensen derives Tir from the Babylonian Dpir = Dipsar, "scribe." However, he overlooks the fact that the East has known and used the word Dpir in an uncorrupted form to this day. Tir may even be regarded as one element in the mysterious Hermes Tresmegisthos, which is usually translated as "Thrice greatest." It seems to be much more natural to say: Hermes, the greatest Tir. However, we have here against us the great army of classical scholars and a hoary tradition.

57. Eznik, pp. 122, 138; also Eghishe, ii. 44. F. Cumont, in his

Mysteries of Mithra, wrongly ascribes these myths to the Armenians themselves, whereas the Armenian authors are only reporting Zrvantian ideas.

58. Greek Agathangelos; Moses, ii. 18.

59. Agathangelos, p. 593. One of the gates of the city of Van is to this day called by Mihr's name (Meher).

60. These human sacrifices may also be explained by Mihr's probable relation to Vahagn. Vahagn is the fierce storm god, who, as in and Teutonic religions, had supplanted the god of the bright heaven. Vahagn may have once required human sacrifices in Armenia; his Teutonic brother Wotan did.

61. Eznik, pp. 15, 16.

Chapter IV

Semitic Deities

SEMITIC deities were introduced into the Armenian pantheon comparatively late, notwithstanding the fact that the Armenians had always been in commercial intercourse with their southern neighbours. It was Tigranes the Great (94-54 B.C.) who brought these gods and goddesses back from his conquests along with their costly statues (1). It is not easy to say how much of politics can be seen in this procedure. As a semi-barbarian, who had acquired a taste for western things, he surely was pleased with the aesthetic show and splendor of the more highly civilized Syrian empire of the Seleucids and its religion. He must have seen also some underlying identity between the Syrian deities and their Armenian brothers. However, in Armenia itself no real fusion took place between the native and foreign gods. The extant records show that out of all the Syrian gods and goddesses who migrated north, only Astghik (Astarte-Aphrodite) obtained a wide popularity. On the contrary, the others became little more than local deities, and that not without at first having encountered fierce opposition. The early stage of things is clearly reflected in the relation of Ba'al Shamin to Vahagn and in the manner in which he figures in the hero stories of Armenia as one who is discomfited or slain in battle. It is becoming more and more certain that almost all of these Semitic gods were brought from Phoenicia. But they hardly can have come in organized, coherent groups like Ba'al Shamin-Astghik as Jensen thinks in his fantastic *Hittiter und Armenier.*

1. Ba'al Shamin (Armen. Barshamina)

In the village of Thortan, where patriarchs descended from Gregory the Illuminator were buried, later stood the "brilliantly white" statue of the Syrian god Ba'al Shamin, the lord of heaven. This statue was made of ivory, crystal, and silver (2). It was a current tradition that Tigranes the Great had captured it during his victorious campaign in Syria. No doubt the costly material was expressive of the character and story of the deity whom it endeavored to portray. In the legendary history of Armenia, where euhemerism rules supreme, Ba'al Shamin appears as a giant whom the Syrians deified on account of his valorous deeds, but who had been vanquished by Aram and slain by his soldiers (3). In reality Ba'al Shamin was originally a supreme god of the heavens, who gave good and evil, life and death, rain and sunshine, but who had already merged his identity in that of the Syrian sun-god, when he came to Armenia. In his adoptive home he ever remained a more or less unpopular rival of Vahagn, a native sun and fire god.

The one genuine Armenian myth about him that has survived is that Vahagn stole straw from him in a cold winter night. The Milky Way was formed from the straw that dropped along as the heavenly thief hurried away (4). This may be a distinctly Armenian but fragmentary version of the Prometheus legend, and the straw may well have something to do with the birth of fire. (See chapter on Vahagn.) Needless to say that the myth which was current even in Christian Armenia was not meant as a compliment to the foreign deity. It was an Armenian god playing a trick on a Syrian intruder. If Astghik was the wife of Ba'al Shamin, Vahagn won another victory over him, by winning her love.

2. Nane (Hanea?)

Nane is undoubtedly the Nana of ancient Babylonia, originally a Sumerian goddess. In Erech (Uruk), a city of South Babylonia, she was the goddess of the evening star and mistress of heaven. In fact, she was simply the Ishtar of Erech, the heroine of the famous Gilgamesh epic, a goddess of the life and activity of nature, of sensual love, of war and of death. Her statue had been in olden times captured by the Elamites, and its return to Erech was celebrated as a great triumph. Her worship in later times had spread broadcast west and north. She was found in Phrygia and even as far as Southern Greece. According to the *First Book of the Maccabees* (Chap. vi, v. 2) her temple at Elam contained golden statues and great treasures.

She may have come to Armenia long before Tigranes enriched the pantheon with Syrian and Phoenician gods. It is difficult to explain how she came to be called the daughter of Aramazd, unless she had once occupied an important position.

We hear nothing about orgiastic rites at her Armenian temple in Thil (the Talia of Ptolemy). On the contrary, in Hellenizing times she was identified with Athene (5), which perhaps means that she had gradually come to be recognised as a wise, austere and war-like goddess.

3. Astghik

Among all the Semitic deities which found their way into the Armenian pantheon, none attained the importance that was acquired by Astghik, especially in Tarauntis. In spite of the presence of Anahit and Nana—two goddesses of her own type and therefore in rivalry with her—she knew how to hold her own and even to win the national god Vahagn as her lover. For her temple at Ashtisat (where Anahit and Vahagn also had famous sanctuaries) was known as "Vahagn's chamber," and in it stood their statues side by side. However it is now impossible to reconstruct the myth that was at the basis of all this. It may be that we have here the intimate relation of a Syrian Ba'al to Astarte. It may also be that the myth is purely Greek and reflects the adventures of Ares with Aphrodite, for Astghik was called Aphrodite by Hellenizing Armenians (6). Hoffman recognized in the Armenian name Astghik (which means "little star") a translation of the Syrian Kaukabhta, a late designation of Ashtart (Ishtar) both as a goddess and as the planet Venus.

The latter is no more called Astghik by the Armenians, but Arusyak, "the little bride," which is an old title of Ishtar, "the veiled bride," and shows that the Armenians not only identified the planet Venus with their goddess Astghik, but were familiar with one of her most important titles.

In view of their essential identity it was natural that some confusion should arise between Astghik and Anahit. So Vanagan Vartabed says: "Astarte is the shame of the Sidonians, whom the Syrians called Kaukabhta, the Greeks Aphrodite, and the Armenians Anahit." Either this medieval author meant to say Astghik instead of Anahit, or for him Astghik's name was not associated with sacred prostitution in Armenia.

The custom of flying doves at the Rose-Sunday of the Armenians in Shirag (see Chapter VIII) suggests a possible relation of Astghik to this festival, the true character of which will be discussed later.

Her memory is still alive in Sassoun (ancient Tarauntis), where young men endeavor to catch a glimpse of the goddess at sunrise when she is bathing in the river. But Astghik, who knows their presence, modestly wraps herself up with the morning mist. Her main temple was at Ashtishat, but she had also other sanctuaries, among which was that at Mount Palat or Pashat.

4. Zatik

The Armenian translation of the Bible calls the Jewish passover "the festival of Zatik," while the Armenian church has from time immemorial applied that name to Easter. Zatik, in the sense of Passover or Easter, is unknown to the Greeks and Syrians. Here occurs, no doubt, an old word for an old deity or an old festival. But what does it mean? The Iberians have a deity called "Zaden," by whom fishermen used to swear, but about whom we know nothing definite except that this deity is feminine and her name probably underlies that of Sathenik, the Albanian queen of King Artaxias (190 B.C.). We may perhaps infer from this queen's reputed devotion to Astghik that Zaden was a northern representative of Ishtar. But Zatik's form and associations remind us of the Palestinian Sedeq = Phoenician *Sgdgk.* It is becoming clearer and clearer that once in Canaan there was such a chief deity whose name occurs in *Melchi-sedeq,* "Sedeq is my King," *Adoni-Sedeq,* "Sedeq is my Lord," or, according to a later view, "Sedeq is King," "Sedeq is Lord." Farther East, the Babylonian Shamash has two sons called respectively Kettu (which, like Sedeq, means "righteousness") and Misharu ("rectitude"). These two deities are mentioned also in the Sanchoniatho fragments of Philo Byblios under the names of Sydyk and Misor, as culture-heroes who have discovered the use of salt. Phoenician inscriptions have Sedeqyathan, "Sedeq gave," as a personal name, as well as combinations of Sedeq with Ramman and Melek. Fr. Jeremias thinks that Sydyk and Misor were respectively the spring and autumn sun in sun-worship and the waxing and waning moon in moon worship.

As twins they were represented by Ashera at the door of Phoenician temples. According to the above mentioned Sanchoniatho fragments, Sydyk was in Phoenicia the father of the seven Kabirs (great gods) and of Eshmun (Asklepios) called the Eighth. In conformity with this in Persian and Greek times Sedeq was recognized among the Syrians as the angel (genius) of the planet Jupiter, an indication that he once was a chief deity. This god may have had also some relation to the Syrian hero-god Sandacos mentioned by Apollodorus of Athens (7), while on the other hand Sandakos may be identified also with the Sanda of Tarsus. At all events Sandakos went to Cilicia and founded (i.e. he was the god of) the city of Celenderis and became through two generations of heroes the father of Adonis. Zatik, as well as Sedeq, was probably a vegetation god, like Adonis, whose resurrection began at the winter solstice and was complete in the spring. The spring festival of such a god would furnish a suitable name both for the Jewish passover and the Christian Easter. The spring celebrations of the death and resurrection of Adonis were often adopted and identified by the Christian churches with the Death and Resurrection of Christ. However, no trace of a regular worship of Zatik is found among the Armenians in historical times, although their Easter celebrations contain a dramatic bewailing, burial, and resurrection of Christ.

Unsatisfactory as this explanation is, it would seem to come nearer the truth than Sandalgian's (supported by Tiryakian and others) identification of Zatik with the Persian root *zad*, "to strike," from which is probably derived the Armenian word *zenum*, " to slaughter."

Footnotes

1. Moses, ii. 14.

2. *Ibid.*, ii. 14.

3. *Ibid.*, i. 14.

4. Anania of Shirag, ed. St. Petersburg, p. 48.

5. *Ibid.*, ii. 14. Greek Agathangelos. Josephus calls the Nana of Elam, Artemis.

6. Moses, ii. 14; Greek Agathangelos.

7. Apollodorus, iii. 14, 3.

Chapter V

Vahagn "The Eighth" God
A National Deity

IN the extant records Vahagn presents himself under the double aspect of a national hero and a god of war or courage (1). A thorough study, however, will show that he was not only a deity but the most national of all the Armenian gods. It is probable that Vahagn was intentionally overlooked when the Armenian pantheon was reorganized according to a stereotyped scheme of seven main "worships." For his official cult is called "the eighth," which probably means that it was an after-thought. Yet once he was recognized, he soon found himself at the very side of Aramazd and Anahit, with whom he formed a triad (2) on the pattern of that of Auramazda, Anahita, and Mithra of the later Persian inscriptions. Moreover, he became a favorite of the Armenian kings who brought sacrifices to his main temple at Ashtishat (3).

How did all this take place? We may venture to suggest that when Zoroastrian ideas of a popular type were pervading Armenia and a Zoroastrian or perhaps Magian pantheon of a fragmentary character was superseding the gods of the country or reducing them to national heroes, Vahagn shared the fate of the latter class. Yet there was so much vitality in his worship, that Mithra himself could not obtain a firm foothold in the land, in the face of the great popularity enjoyed by this native rival.

Moses of Khoren reports an ancient song about Vahagn's birth, which will give us the surest clue to his nature and origin. It reads as follows:

The heavens and the earth travailed,
There travailed also the purple sea,
The travail held
The red reed (4) (stalk) in the sea.
Through the hollow of the reed (stalk) a smoke rose,
Through the hollow of the reed (stalk) a flame rose
And out of the flame ran forth a youth.
He had hair of fire,
He had a beard of flame,
And his eyes were suns.

Other parts of this song, now lost, said that Vahagn had fought
and conquered dragons. Vishapakagh, "dragon-reaper," was his
best known title. He was also invoked, at least in royal edicts,
as a god of courage. It is mostly in this capacity that he became
a favorite deity with the Armenian kings, and in later
syncretistic times, was identified with Herakles. Besides these
attributes Vahagn claimed another. He was a sun-god. A
medieval writer says that the sun was worshipped by the
ancients under the name of Vahagn (5), and his rivalry with
Ba'al Shamin and probably also with Mihr, two other sun-gods
of a foreign origin, amply confirms this explicit testimony.

These several and apparently unconnected reports about
Vahagn, put together, evoke the striking figure of a god which
can be paralleled only by the Vedic Agni, the fire-god who forms
the fundamental and original unity underlying the triad:—
Indra, the lightning, Agni, the universal and sacrificial fire, and
Surya, the sun. Besides the fact that Vahagn's name may very
well be a compound of Vah and Agni, no better commentary on
the birth, nature and functions of Vahagn may be found than
the Vedic songs on these three deities.

From the above quoted fragment which was sung to the
accompaniment of the lyre by the bards of Goghthn (6) long
after the Christianization of Armenia, we gather that Vahagn's
birth had a universal significance. He was a son of heaven,
earth, and sea, but more especially of the sea. This wonderful
youth may be the sun rising out of the sea, but more probably
he is the fire-god surging out of the heavenly sea in the form of
the lightning, because the travail can be nothing else than the

raging storm. However, this matters little, for in Aryan religion, the sun is the heavenly fire and only another aspect of Agni. It is very significant that Armenians said both of the setting sun and of the torch that went out, that "they were going to their mother," i.e. they returned to the common essence from which they were born. Once we recognize the unity of all fire in heaven, in the skies, and on earth, as the Vedas do, we need no more consider the universal travail at Vahagn's birth as a poetic fancy of the old Armenian bards. Here we are on old Aryan ground. At least in the Rgveda the fire claims as complex a parenthood as Vahagn. It is the child of heaven, earth, and water (7). Even the description of the external appearance of the Vedic Agni (and of Indra himself) agrees with that of Vahagn. Agni is always youthful, like Vahagn, with a continual fresh birth. Agni (as well as Indra) has tawny hair and beard like Vahagn, who has "hair of fire and beard of flame." Surya, the sun, is Agni's eye. Vahagn's eyes are suns.

However, the key to the situation is the "reed" or "stalk." It is a very important word in Indo-European mythology in connection with fire in its three forms, sun, lightning, and earthly fire. It is the specially sacred fuel which gives birth to the sacred fire. The Greek culture-hero Prometheus brought down the fire stolen from the gods (or the sun) in a fennel stalk. Indra, the lightning-god of the Vedas, after killing Vrtra was seized with fear and hid himself for a while in the stalk of a lotus flower in a lake. Once Agni hid himself in the water and in plants, where the gods finally discovered him. The sage Atharvan (8) of the Vedas extracted Agni from the lotus flower, i.e. from the lotus stalk. Many dragon-killers, who usually have some relation to the fire, sun, or lightning, are born out of an enchanted flower (9). We must regard it as a very interesting and significant echo of the same hoary myth that Zarathustra's soul was sent down in the stalk of a haoma-plant. Such a righteous soul was no doubt conceived as a fiery substance derived from above.

It is not more than reasonable to see one original and primitive myth at the root of all these stories, the myth of the miraculous birth of the one universal fire stolen from the sun or produced by the fire-drill in the clouds whence it comes down to the earth (see Chapter VII). Further, the dragon-slaying of ancient mythology is usually the work of fire in one or another of its three aspects. The Egyptian sun-god (evidently a compound being) kills the dragon through his fire-spitting serpents. The *Atar* of the Avesta (who gives both heat and light) fights with Azi Dahaka. The Greek Herakles, manifestly a sun-god, strangles serpents in his early childhood. Agni, as well as Indra and Surya, is a Vrtra-slayer. Nothing scares away the Macedonian dragon so successfully as the name of the thunderbolt, and it is well known how the evil spirits of superstition and folklore, which are closely allied with dragons, as we shall see, are always afraid of fire-brands and of fire in general. Macdonell says that Agni is very prominent as a goblin-slayer, even more so than Indra.

Finally, Vahagn's attributes of courage and victory are not strangers to the Vedic Agni and Indra (10). Both of them are gods of war and victory, no doubt mostly in virtue of their meteorological character. The war-like nature of weather-gods is a commonplace of universal mythology. Even the Avestic Verethraghna inherits this distinctive quality from his original Indo-European self, when his name was only a title of Indra or Vayu. We purposely delayed the mention of one point in our general description of Vahagn. Modern Armenian folklore knows a storm god called *Dsovean* (sea-born), who with an angry storm goddess, *Dsovinar* (she who was born of the sea), rules supreme in the storm and often appears to human eyes (11). In view of the fact that we do not know any other sea-born deity in Armenian mythology, who else could this strange figure of folklore be but Vahagn, still killing his dragons in the sky with his fiery sword or arrow and sending down the fertilizing rain? His title "sea-born," which must have been retained from an ancient usage and is in perfect keeping with the extant Vahagn song, strongly recalls the Vedic *Apam napat* "water child," who is supreme in the seas, dispensing water to mankind, but also identical with Agni clad with the lightning in the clouds (12). Dsovinar may very well be a reminiscence of the mermaids who accompanied the "water-child," or even some female goddess like Indrani, the wife of Indra. From these considerations it becomes very plain that Vahagn is a fire and lightning god, born out of the stalk (13) in the heavenly (?) sea, with the special mission among other beneficent missions, to slay dragons. His title of dragon-reaper is a distant but unmistakable echo of a pre-Vedic Vrtrahan. In fact, the Armenian myth about him is an independent tradition from the original home of the Indo-Iranians, and confirms the old age of many a Vedic myth concerning Agni, which modern scholars tend to regard as the fancies of later poets (14). And is it not a striking coincidence that the only surviving fragment about Vahagn should be a birth-song, a topic which, according to Macdonell, has, along with the sacrificial functions of Agni, a paramount place in the minds of the Vedic singers of Agni (15)?

Footnotes

1. *Ibid.*, i. 31 : Agathangelos, pp. 106, 607.

2. Agathangelos, p. 106.

3. *Ibid.*, p. 606.

4. The Armenian word for "reed" is *egheg*. The Phrygian cognate of *egheg* is probably at the root of the Greek *elegeion* "elegy," which originally had nothing to do with elegiac poetry, but a doleful melody accompanied by the flute. The relation of the reed to the flute is well known to those who are familiar with the myths of Pan. Armenian also possesses the word *egher* in the sense of "dirge" (see F. B. Jevons, *History of Greek Literature*, New York, 1886, p. III), but *egher* has nothing to do with "elegy."

5. Alishan, p. 87.

6. The district of Goghthn seems to have clung to the old paganism more tenaciously than any other in Armenia.

7. All these facts are recognized and clearly expressed by Oldenberg, p. 105 f.; Lehmann, in P. D. Chantepie de la Saussaye, *Lehrbuch* ii. 27; Macdonell, at 35; Moore, i. 254 f.

46

8. There is a great temptation to connect Aravan, the son of (Moses, i, 31), with this Vedic priest, as some have already connected the Bhrgu of the Vedas with Brig = Phrygians. Atharvan could easily pass to Aravan through Ahrvan. However, the name is also Avestic.

9. Chhalatianz, p. xiii. Even in Egyptian mythology the Sun-god is sometimes born out of an egg, but he is born also out of the lotus-stalk or he is said to have spent his childhood in the lotus flower. Cf. *Mythology of All Races*, Boston, 1918, xii. 25, 50.

10. Macdonell, pp. 89, 98.

11. Abeghian, p. 83 f. It is a very strange and significant coincidence that in the Veda also the sea-born Agni is related to the lightning (*Rig-veda-Sanhita: a collection of ancient Hindu Hymns*, tr. H. H. Wilson, London, 1850-88, vi. 119, note), and that Agni gives rain (*Ibid.*, p. 387). Cf. also Oldenberg, p. 167 f.; Macdonell, at 35, where the sea is identified with the heavenly sea.

12. Oldenberg, p. 120.

13. We would suggest that this is the origin of the use of *baresman* both in India and in Iran at the worship of the fire and of the *baresman* at the Magian worship of the sun. The grass or stalk cushion upon which the sacrifice is laid and the bunch of green stalks or twigs held before the face were perhaps supposed to be an effective charm, meant to work favorably upon the sun and the fire.

14. Sandalgian's theory that Vahagn came to Armenia straight from Vedic India has no sound foundation.

15. See Appendix, I, Vahagn.

Chapter VI

Nature Worship and Nature Myths

1. Sun, Moon, and Stars

MOSES of Chorene makes repeated allusions to the worship of the sun and moon in Armenia. In oaths the name of the sun was almost invariably invoked (1), and there were also altars and images of the sun and moon (2). Of what type these images were, and how far they were influenced by Syrian or Magian sun-worship, we cannot tell. We shall presently see the medieval conceptions of the forms of the sun and moon. Modern Armenians imagine the sun to be like the wheel of a water-mill (3). Agathangelos, in the alleged letter of Diocletian to Tiridates, unconsciously bears witness to the Armenian veneration for the sun, moon and stars (4). But the oldest witness is Xenophon, who notes that the Armenians sacrificed horses to the sun (5), perhaps with some reference to his need of them in his daily course through the skies. The eighth month of the Armenian year and, what is more significant, the first day of every month, were consecrated to the sun and bore its name, while the twenty-fourth day in the Armenian month was consecrated to the moon. The Armenians, like the Persians and most of the sun-worshipping peoples of the East, prayed toward the rising sun, a custom which the early church adopted, so that to this day the Armenian churches are built and the Armenian dead are buried toward the east, the west being the abode of evil spirits. As to the moon, Ohannes Mantaguni in the Fifth Century bears witness to the belief that the moon prospers or mars the plants (6), and Anania of Shirak says in his *Demonstrations* (7) "The first fathers called her the nurse of the plants," a quite widely spread idea which has its parallel, both in the west and in the short Mah-yasht of the Avesta, particularly in the statement that vegetation grows best in the time of the waxing moon (8). At certain of its phases the moon caused diseases, especially epilepsy, which was called the moon-disease, and Eznik tries to combat this superstition with the explanation that it is caused by demons whose activity is connected with the phases of the moon (9)! The modem Armenians are still very much afraid of the baleful influence of the moon upon children and try to ward it off by magical ceremonies in the presence of the moon (10).

As among many other peoples, the eclipse of the sun and moon was thought to be caused by dragons which endeavor to swallow these luminaries. But the "evil star" of the Western Armenians is a plain survival of the superstitions current among the Persians, who held that these phenomena were caused by two dark bodies, offspring of the primaeval ox, revolving below the sun and moon, and occasionally passing between them and the earth (11). When the moon was at an eclipse, the sorcerers said that it resembled a demon (?). It was, moreover, a popular belief that a sorcerer could bind the sun and moon in their course, or deprive them of their light. He could bring the sun or moon down from heaven by witchcraft and although it was larger than many countries (worlds?) put together, the sorcerers could set the moon in a threshing floor, and although without breasts, they could milk it like a cow (12). This latter point betrays some reminiscence of a primaeval cow in its relation to the moon and perhaps shows that this luminary was regarded by the Armenians also as a goddess of fertility. Needless to add that the eclipses and the appearance of comets foreboded evil. Their chronologies are full of notices of such astronomical phenomena that presaged great national and universal disasters. Along with all these practices, there was a special type of divination by the moon.

Both sun and moon worship have left deep traces in the popular beliefs of the present Armenians (13).

A few ancient stellar myths have survived, in a fragmentary condition. Orion, Sirius, and other stars were perhaps involved

49

in myths concerning the national hero, Hayk, as they bear his name.

We have seen that Vahagn's stealing straw from Ba'al Shamin and forming the Milky Way, has an unmistakable reference to his character. The Milky Way itself was anciently known as "the Straw-thief's Way," and the myth is current among the Bulgarians, who may have inherited it from the ancient Thracians.

Some of the other extant sun-myths have to do with the great luminary's travel beyond the western horizon. The setting sun has always been spoken of among the Armenians and among Slavs as the sun that is going to his mother. According to Frazer "Stesichorus also described the sun embarking in a golden goblet that he might cross the ocean in the darkness of night and come to his mother, his wedded wife and children dear." The sun may, therefore, have been imagined as a young person, who, in his resplendent procession through the skies, is on his way to a re-incarnation. The people probably believed in a daily occurrence of death and birth, which the sun, as the heavenly fire, has in common with the fire, and which was most probably a return into a heavenly stalk or tree and reappearance from it. This heavenly stalk or tree itself must therefore have been the mother of the sun, as well as of the fire, and in relation to the sun was known to the Letts and even to the ancient Egyptians. The Armenians have forgotten the original identity of the mother of the sun and have produced other divergent accounts of which Abeghian has given us several (15), They often think the dawn or the evening twilight to be the mother of the sun. She is a brilliant woman with eyes shining like the beams of the sun and with a golden garment, who bestows beauty upon the maidens at sunset. Now she is imagined as a good woman helping those whom the sun punished, now as a bad woman cursing and changing men into stone. The mother of the sun is usually supposed to reside in the palace of the sun, which is either in the east at the end of the world or in a sea, like the Lake of Van. In the absence of a sea, there is at least a basin near the mother. Like the Letto-Lithuanians, who thought that Perkuna Tete, the mother of the thunder and lightning, bathes the sun, and refreshes him at the end of the day, the Armenians also associate this mother closely with the bath which the sun takes at the close of his daily journey. The palace itself is gorgeously described. It is situated in a far-off place where there are no men, no birds, no trees, and no turf, and where the great silence is disturbed only by the murmur of springs welling up in the middle of each one of the twelve courts, which are built of blue marble and spanned over by arches. In the middle court, over the spring, there is a pavilion where the mother of the sun waits for him, sitting on the edge of a pearl bed among lights. When he returns he bathes in the spring, is taken up, laid in bed and nursed by his mother.

Further, that the sun crosses a vast sea to reach the east was also known to the Armenians. Eznik is trying to prove that this is a myth but that the sun passes underneath the earth all the same. The sea is, of course, the primaeval ocean upon which the earth was founded. It is on this journey that the sun shines on the Armenian world of the dead as he did on the Babylonian Aralu and on the Egyptian and Greek Hades. The following extract from an Armenian collection of folklore unites the sun's relation to Hades and to the subterranean ocean: "And at sunset the sun is the *portion* of the dead. It enters the sea and, passing under the earth, emerges in the morning at the other side " (16).

Medieval writers (17) speak about the horses of the sun, an idea which is no more foreign to the Persians than to the Greeks. One counts four of them, and calls them Enik, Menik, Benik, and Senik, which sound like artificial or magic names, but evidently picture the sun on his quadriga. Another, mingling the scientific ideas of his time with mythical images, says: "The sun is a compound of fire, salt, and iron, light blended with lightning, fire that has been shaped—or with a slight emendation—fire drawn by horses. There are in it twelve windows with double shutters, eleven of which look upward, and one to the earth. Wouldst thou know the shape of the sun? It is that of a man deprived of reason and speech standing between two horses. If its eye (or its real essence) were not in a dish, the world would blaze up before it like a mass of wool."

51

The reader will readily recognize in "the windows of the sun " a far-off echo of early Greek philosophy.

Ordinarily in present-day myths the sun is thought to be a young man and the moon a young girl. But, on the other hand, the Germanic idea of a feminine sun and masculine moon is not foreign to Armenian thought. They are brother and sister, but sometimes also passionate lovers who are engaged in a weary search for each other through the trackless fields of the heavens. In such cases it is the youthful moon who is pining away for the sun-maid. Bashfulness is very characteristic of the two luminaries, as fair maids. So the sun hurls fiery needles at the bold eyes which presume to gaze upon her face, and the moon covers hers with a sevenfold veil of clouds (18). These very transparent and poetic myths, however, have little in them that might be called ancient.

The ancient Armenians, like the Latins, possessed two different names for the moon. One of these was *Lusin*, an unmistakable cognate of *Luna* (originally *Lucna* or *Lucina*), and the other *Ami(n)s*, which now like the Latin mens, signifies "month." No doubt *Lusin* designated the moon as a female goddess, while *Amins* corresponded to the Phrygian *men* or *Lunus*. ·

The same mediaeval and quasi-scientific author who gives the above semi-mythological description of the sun, portrays the moon in the following manner: "The moon was made out of five parts, three of which are light, the fourth is fire, and the fifth, motion...which is a compound. It is cloud-like, light-like (luminous) dense air, with twelve windows, six of which look heavenward and six earthward. What are the forms of the moon? In it are two sea-buffaloes (?). The light enters into the mouth of the one and is waning in the mouth of the other. For the light of the moon comes from the sun" (19). Here again the sea-buffaloes may be a dim and confused reminiscence of a "primaeval cow" which was associated with the moon and, no doubt, suggested by the peculiar form of the crescent. Let us add also that the Armenians spoke of the monthly rebirth of the moon, although myths concerning it are lacking.

Fragments of Babylonian star-lore found their way into Armenia probably through Median Magi. We have noticed the planetary basis of the pantheon. In later times, however, some of the planets came into a bad repute (20). Anania of Shirak (seventh century) reports that heathen (?) held Jupiter and Venus to be beneficent, Saturn and Mars were malicious, but Mercury was indifferent.

Stars and planets and especially the signs of the Zodiac were bound up with human destiny upon which they exercised a decisive influence. According to Eznik (21) the Armenians believed that these heavenly objects caused births and deaths. Good and ill luck were dependent upon the entrance of certain stars into certain signs of the Zodiac. So they said: "When Saturn is in the ascendant, a king dies; when Leo (the lion) is ascendant, a king is born. When the Taurus is ascendant, a powerful and good person is born. With Aries, a rich person is born, ' just as the ram has a thick fleece.' With the Scorpion, a wicked and sinful person comes to the world. Whoever is born when Hayk (Mars?) is in the ascendant dies by iron, i.e., the sword." Much of this star lore is still current among the Mohammedans in a more complete form.

Eznik alludes again and again to the popular belief that stars, constellations, and Zodiacal signs which bear names of animals like Sirius (dog), Arcturus (bear), were originally animals of those names that have been lifted up into the heavens.

Something of the Armenian belief in the influence that Zodiacal signs could exercise on the weather and crops is preserved by al-Biruni (22) where we read: "I heard a number of Armenian learned men relate that on the morning of the Fox-day there appears on the highest mountain, between the Interior and the Exterior country, a white ram (Aries?) which is not seen at any other time of the year except about this time of this Day. Now the inhabitants of that country infer that the year will be prosperous if the ram bleats; that it will be sterile if it does not bleat."

FIG. 1. RELIEF

Found in the neighborhood of Ezzinjan

Footnotes

1. Moses, ii. 19.

2. *Ibid.*, ii. 77. The modern Armenian use of the word "sun" in the sense of "life," is due perhaps to the fact that the sun brings the day, and days make up the sum of human life.

3. Abeghian, p. 41.

4. Agathangelos, p. 125.

5. Xenophon, *Anab.*, iv. 5. 35.

6. *Discourses*, Venice, 1860, p. 198-9.

7. Ed. Patkanean, p. 66.

8. *Yasht*, vii. 4; Al-Biruni, *Chron.*, p. 219.

9. Eznik, p. 180.

10. Abeghian, p. 49.

11. *Dadistan-i Dinik*, lxix. 2; *Sikand-Gumanik Vijar*, iv. 46.

12. Eznik, p. 217. See also Appendix II, Witchcraft and Magic.

13. Abeghian, pp. 4-1-49; Tcheraz, in TICO ii. 823 f.

14. Alishan, in one of his popular poems, calls the Milky Way the manger from which the dragon may break loose. This is the echo of some myth which we have not been able to locate. A modern Armenian legend says that the Milky Way was formed by two brothers who worked together in the fields and then divided the crop on the threshing-floor. One of them was married and the other single. In the night the married one would rise and carry sheaves from his stack to his brother's, saying, "My brother is single and needs some conolation." The other would do the same, saying, "My brother is narried and needs help." Thus going to and fro they scattered the dtraw.

15. Abeghian, pp. 41-4-5.

16. Pshrank, p. 198.

17. Alishan, p. 89.

18. Abeghian, p. 4-5; Pshrank, p. 198.

19. Quoted by Alishan, p. 98.

20. It is well known how later Zoroastrianism degraded the genii of all the planets in demoniac powers.

21. Eznik, p. 153 f.

22. Al-Biruni, *Chron.*, p. 211.

Chapter VII

Nature Worship and Nature Myths

2. Fire

THE worship of fire was possessed by Armenians as a venerable heirloom long before they came into contact with Zoroastrianism. It was so deeply rooted that the Christian authors do not hesitate to call the heathen Armenians ash-worshippers, a name which they apply also to the Persians with less truth. We have seen that the old word "Agni" was known to the Armenians in the name of Vahagn and that their ideas of the fire-god were closely akin to those of the Rgveda. Fire was, for them, the substance of the sun and of the lightning. Fire gave heat and also light. Like the sun, the light-giving fire had a "mother," most probably the water-born and water-fed stalk or tree out of which fire was, obtained by friction or otherwise (1). To this mother the fire returned when extinguished. Even today to put out a candle or a fire is not a simple matter, but requires some care and respect. Fire must not be desecrated by the presence of a dead body, by human breath, by spitting into it, or burning in it such unclean things as hair and parings of the finger nail. An impure fire must be rejected and a purer one kindled in its place, usually from a flint. All this may be Zoroastrian but it is in perfect accord with the older native views.

The people swear by the hearth-fire just as also by the sun. Fire was and still is the most potent means of driving the evil spirits away. The Eastern Armenian who will bathe in the night scares away the malignant occupants of the lake or pool by casting a fire-brand into it, and the man who is harassed by an obstinate demon has no more powerful means of getting rid of him than to strike fire out of a flint. Through the sparks that the latter apparently contains, it has become, along with iron (2), an important weapon against the powers of darkness. Not only evil spirits but also diseases, often ascribed to demoniac influences, can not endure the sight of fire, but must flee before this mighty deity. In Armenian there are two words for fire. One is *hur* (3), a cognate of the Greek *pur*, and the other *krak*, probably derived, like the other Armenian word *jrag*, "candle," "light," from the Persian *cirag* (also *cirah*, *carag*). *Hur* was more common in ancient Armenian, but we find also *krak* as far back as the Armenian literature reaches. While Vahagn is unmistakably a male deity, we find that the fire as a deity was female, like Hestia or Vesta. This was also true of the Scythian fire-god whom Herodotus calls Hestia. On the contrary the Vedic Agni and the Avestic Atar were masculine.

The worship of fire took among the Armenians a two-fold aspect. There was first the hearth-worship. This seems to have been closely associated with ancestor spirits (4), which naturally flocked around the center and symbol of the home-life. It is the lips of this earthen and sunken fireplace which the young bride reverently kisses with the groom, as she enters her new home for the first time. And it is around it that they piously circle three times. A brand from this fire will be taken when any member of the family goes forth to found a new home. Abeghian, from whose excellent work on the popular beliefs of the Armenians we have culled some of this material, says that certain villages have also their communal hearth, that of the founder of the village, etc., which receives something like general reverence, and often, in cases of marriage and baptism, is a substitute for a church when there is none at hand. Ethnologists who hold that the development of the family is later than that of the community would naturally regard the communal fire as prior in order and importance.

A very marked remnant of hearth and ancestor worship is found in special ceremonies like cleaning the house thoroughly and burning candles and incense, which takes place everywhere on Saturdays.

The second aspect of fire-worship in Armenia is the public one.

It is true that the Persian Atrushans (fire-temples or enclosures) found little favor in both heathen and Christian Armenia, and that fire, as such, does not seem to have attained a place in the rank of the main deities. Nevertheless, there was a public fire-worship, whether originally attached to a communal hearth or not. It went back sometimes to a Persian *frobag* or *farnbag* (Arm. *hurbak*) fire, and in fact we have several references to a Persian or Persianized fire-altar in Bagavan, the town of the gods (5). Moreover, there can be little doubt that Armenians joined the Persians in paying worship to the famous seven fire-springs of Baku in their old province of Phaitakaran. But usually the Armenian worship of the fire possessed a native character.

The following testimonies seem to describe some phases of this widely spread and deeply rooted national cult.

In the hagiography called the "Coming of the Rhipsimean Virgins" (6) wrongly ascribed to Moses of Chorene, we read that on the top of Mount Palat (?) there was a house of Aramazd and Astghik (Venus), and on a lower peak, to the southeast, there was "a house of fire, of insatiable fire, the god of incessant combustion." At the foot of the mountain, moreover, there was a mighty spring. The place was called Buth. "They burnt the Sister Fire and the Brother Spring."

Elsewhere we read, in like manner: "Because they called the fire sister, and the spring brother, they did not throw the ashes away, but they wiped them with the tears of the brother (7). Lazare of Pharpe, a writer of the fifth century (8), speaking of an onslaught of the Christian Armenians on the sacred fire, which the Persians were endeavoring to introduce into Armenia, says: "They took the fire and carried it into the water as into the bosom of her brother, according to the saying of the false teachers of the Persians." The latter part of his statement, however, is mistaken. So far as we know, the Persians did not cast the sacred fire into the water, but allowed the ashes to be heaped in the fire enclosure. When the floating island (sea-monster) upon which Keresaspa had unwittingly kindled a fire, sank and the fire fell into the water, this was accounted to him a great sin. The above was rather a purely Armenian rite. It would seem that it was a part of the Armenian worship of the Sister Fire to extinguish her in the bosom of her loving brother, the water, a rite which certainly hides some nature myth, like the relation of the lightning to the rain, or like the birth of the fire out of the stalk in the heavenly sea. Whatever the real meaning of this procedure was, the ashes of the sacred fire imparted to the water with which they were "wiped" healing virtue. Even now in Armenia, for example, in Agn and Diarbekir the sick are given this potent medicine to drink which consists of the flaky ashes of oak-fire mixed with water. W. Caland reports the same custom of the ancient Letts in his article on the Pre-Christian Death and Burial Rites of the Baltic People (9). As the oak in the European world is the tree sacred to the god of the heavens and the storm, we may easily perceive what underlies the ancient custom.

But it is not clear whether the Armenians (like many Western nations) had several fire-festivals in the year. We have, however, the survival of an indubitable fire-festival—which originally aimed at influencing the activity of the rain-god—in the annual bonfire kindled everywhere by Armenians at Candlemas, or the Purification of the Blessed Virgin, on the 13th of February, in the courts of the churches. The fuel often consists of stalks, straw, and thistles, which are kindled from a candle of the altar (10). The bonfire is usually repeated on the streets, in the house-yards, or on the flat roofs. The people divine the future crops through the direction of the flames and smoke. They leap over it (as a lustration?) and circle around it. Sometimes also they have music and a dance. The ashes are often carried to the fields to promote their fertility. It is perhaps not entirely without significance that this festival falls within the month of Mehekan (consecrated to Mihr), as the Armenian Mithra had distinctly become a fire-god (11). Another fire-festival, rather locally observed, will be mentioned in the next chapter.

59

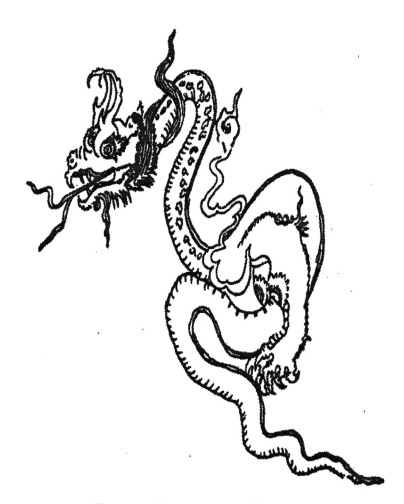

FIG. 2. DRAGON-LIKE FIGURE

Footnotes

1. Here it is worth while to notice how Kuhn in his exhaustive tudy of fire-myths, called *Die Herabkunft des Feuers*, Gutersloh 886, summarizes his conclusion. He says (p.35): "The myths which have just been compared show the same belief among the Indians, Greeks, and Italians in regard to the fact that the earthly fire has been brought to mankind as a heavenly spark in (the form of) the lightning by a semi-

divine being who was originally (and) generally imagined as a winged being, as a bird. The people must have thought that the spark is produced in the clouds by twirling, just in le same manner as they saw the fire gotten out of the primeval instrument, through a circling friction."

2. Possibly the fear with which iron is supposed to inspire evil spirits is also due to the fact of its containing and producing sparks like the flint. A curious passage of the 1st Book of Jalal ad-Din-ar-Rumi's *Mathnavi* makes much of the fire which iron and stone contain, and which may not be extinguished by water.

3. Aspirated "p" became "h" in Armenian, as "pater," Armen, *hayr*. The Phrygian word for fire is said by Plato to have resembled the Greek *pur*.

4. In many places these ancestral spirits have become just spirits: idefined and general.

5. There were in Armenia at least three towns of the gods: Bagayarij in Derzanes, Bagavan in Bagrevand, and Bagaran on the river Akhurean. See H. Hubschmann, *Die Altarmen. Ortsnamen*, pp. 410-11.

6. Alishan, *Hayapatum*, p. 79.

7. "Story of the Picture of the Holy Virgin," in Moses of Chorene.

8. Lazare of Pharpe (5th cent.), p. 203.

9. ARW xvii. [1914] 479. Similar customs are reported also of the Belgians. See Frazer, *GB*, part 7, *Balder the Beautiful* London, i. 194 f.

10. Many of the German sacred fire-festivals were also taken under the patronage of the church and started from a candle (Kuhn, *Die Herabkunft des Feuers* p. 41 f.).

11. See Frazer, *GB*, pt. 7, *Balder the Beautiful*, i. 131, for a very interesting and fuller account of the Armenian New Fires at Candlemas. In fact the whole Chapter V constitutes the richest material on new fires and the best treatment of this subject. Notice that securing fruitfulness, for the fields, trees, animals, etc., is the chief motive of the fires, but next comes the desire to prevent disease. These fires were

intended to exert some favorable influence on the fire-god in general and on the lightning (rain) god in particular. The February fires in England, which were kindled on Candlemas, if productive of bad weather, heralded thereby the coming of the rainy season, i.e. the spring. For in this sense alone it is possible to understand the old English verses:

"If Candlemas be dry and fair
The half o' winter's to come and mair;
If Candlemas be wet and foul
The half o' winter's gane at Yule."

See also artt. "Feu" in *La Grande Encyclopedie*; "Fire" in *EB*; "Candlemas" in *ERE* iii. 189 f.

Chapter VIII

Nature Worship and Nature Myths

3. Water

IF fire were a female principle, water was masculine, and as we
have noticed, they were somehow very closely associated as
sister and brother in the Armenian fire-worship. It is possible
that this kinship was suggested by the trees and luxuriant
verdure growing on the banks of rivers and lakes. As we know,
reeds grew even in the heavenly sea.

Many rivers and springs were sacred, and endowed with
beneficent virtues. According to Tacitus (1), the Armenians
offered horses as a sacrifice to the Euphrates, and divined by
its waves and foam. The sources of the Euphrates and Tigris
received and still receive worship (2). Sacred cities were built
around the river Araxes and its tributaries. Even now there are
many sacred springs with healing power, usually called "the
springs of light," and the people always feel a certain veneration
towards water in motion, which they fear to pollute. The people
still drink of these ancient springs and burn candles and
incense before them, for they have placed them under the
patronage of Christian saints.

The Transfiguration Sunday, which comes in June, was
connected by the Armenian Church with an old water festival.
At this time people drench each other with water and the
ecclesiastical procession throws rose water at the congregation
during the Transfiguration Day rites. On this day the churches
are richly decorated with roses and the popular name of the
Festival is *Vartavar*, "Burning with Roses" (3).

63

It is also reported that in various parts of Armenia, the *Vartavar* is preceded by a night of bonfires. Therefore it can be nothing else than the water festival which seems to have once gone hand in hand with the midsummer (St. John's, St. Peter's, etc.) fires in Europe, at which roses played a very conspicuous part (4). It is barely possible that the Armenian name of this festival, "Burning with Roses," preserves some allusion to the original but now missing fire, and even that flowers were burnt in it or at least cast across the fire as in Europe. In Europe the midsummer water festival was observed also with bathings and visits to sacred springs. In parts of Germany straw wheels set on fire were quenched in the river; and in Marseilles, the people drenched each other with water. There can be little doubt that the water was used in these various ways not only as a means of purification from guilt and disease, but also and principally as a rain-charm. Frazer, who, in his *Golden Bough*, has heaped together an enormous mass of material on the various elements and aspects of these festivals, has thereby complicated the task of working out a unified and self-consistent interpretation.

The custom of throwing water at each other is reported by al-Biruni (5) of the Persians, in connection with their New Year's festival. As the Persian new year came in the spring, there can be little doubt that the festival aimed at the increase of the rain by sympathetic magic (6). In fact, even now in certain places of Armenia the tillers returning from their first day of labour in the fields are sprinkled with water by those who lie in wait for them on the way. So it may be safely assumed that in Armenia also in ancient times the Navasard brought with it the first water-festival of the year. In certain places like the region of Shirak, flying doves form a part of the Vartavar celebrations. Whether this has some reference to an old Astghik (Ishtar) festival, is difficult to say. It is quite possible that as in Europe, so also in ancient Armenia, love-making and other more objectionable rites, formed an important feature of these mid-summer celebrations.

The great centre of the Armenian Navasard and of the water festival (Vartavar) was Bagavan, probably because both had the same character. The fact that Bagavan was also a centre of fire-worship emphasizes once more the close association of these two elements which we have already pointed out.

Footnotes

1. *Annals* vi. 37.

2. Lehmann, "Religionsgesch. aus Kaukasien und Armenien," in ARW, iii. [1900] 4 f.

3. There are those who have explained Vartavar from the Sanscrit as meaning "sprinkling with water," and it can possibly mean also "increasing the waters." However befitting, this Sanscrit etymology is far-fetched.

4. For the numerous references on this subject, see the General Index of Frazer's *Golden Bough* under "Fire," "Water," etc. It would be worth while to inquire also whether the Roman Rosalia (*Rosales esces*) and the Slavic and Macedonian Rousalia are in any way related to the Armenian Vartavar. See G. F. Abbott, *Macedonian Folk-lore* Cambridge, 1903, pp. 40 ff. These western festivals, however, come much earlier.

5. Al-Biruni, *Chron.*, pp. 199, 203.

6. The Armenians had other methods of fire-making.

Chapter IX

Nature Worship and Nature Myths

4. Trees, Plants, and Mountains

WE HAVE old testimony to tree and plant worship in Armenia. There were first the poplars (*sausi*) of Armenia, by which a legendary *saus* (whose name and existence were probably derived from the venerated tree itself) divined. Then we have the words *Haurut, Maurut*, as names of flowers (*Hyacinthus racemosus Dodonei*). These, however, seem to be an echo of the Iranian Haurvatat and Ameretat ("health" and "immortality"), two Amesha-Spentas who were also the genii of plants and water. The oak and other trees are still held to be sacred, especially those near a spring, and upon these one may see hanging pieces of clothing from persons who wish to be cured of some disease. This practice is often explained as a substitution of a part for the whole, and it is very common also among the Semites in general and the Mohammedans in particular (1).

Many mountains were sacred, while others, perhaps sacred by themselves in very ancient times, became the sites of famous temples. The towering Massis (Ararat) was called Azat (Yazata?), "venerable." It was a seat of dragons and fairies, but the main reason of its sacredness must be sought in its imposing grandeur, its volcanic character, or even its association with some deity like Marsyas-Masses, by the Phrygo-Armenians (2). This Phrygian god Marsyas-Masses was famous for his skill with the flute but especially for his widely known interest in rivers. He was the son of Hyagnis, probably a lightning god, and like the Norwegian Agne was hung from a tree by Apollo, who skinned him alive (Apuleius). In fact Marsyas was no more than a tribal variety of Hyagnis, and Hyagnis can be nothing else but the Phrygian form of Vahagn.

Mount Npat (xxx of Strabo), the source of the mighty Tigris, must have enjoyed some veneration as a deity, because the 26th day of each Armenian month was dedicated to it. It has been maintained that Npat was considered by Zoroastrians the seat of Apam-Napat, an important Indo-Iranian water deity.

Mt. Pashat or Palat was the seat of an Aramazd and Astghik temple and a centre of flre-worship. Another unidentified mountain in Sophene was called the Throne of Anahit.

One may safely assume that the Armenians thought in an animistic way, and saw in these natural objects of worship some god or spirit who in Christian times easily assumed the name and character of a saint.

Footnotes

1. Abeghian, p. 59 f.; Lehmann, "Religionsgeschichte aus Kaukasien und Armenien," in ARW, iii. [1900] 10 f.

2. The name Massis for this snow-capped giant of Armenia seems to have been unknown to the old Urartians. It may be an Armenian importation, if not a later Northern echo of the Massios, which was in Assyrian times the name of the great mountain in the plain of Diarbekir. According to Nicholas of Damascus (see Josephus, *Ant.* I. iii. 6) this mountain was known also by the name of *Baris*, which Sandalgian compares with the Sacred mountain *Hara-berezaiti* of the Avesta.

Chapter X

Heroes

THE loss of the ancient songs of Armenia is especially regrettable at this point, because they concerned themselves mostly with the purely national gods and heroes. The first native writers of Armenian history, having no access to the ancient Assyrian, Greek, and Latin authors, drew upon this native source for their material. Yet the old legends were modified or toned down in accordance with euhemeristic views and accommodated to Biblical stories and Greek chronicles, especially that of Eusebius of Caesarea. It is quite possible that the change had already begun in pagan times, when Iranian and Semitic gods made their conquest of Armenia.

1. Hayk

There can be little doubt that the epic songs mentioned Hayk first of all. Hayk was a handsome giant with finely proportioned limbs, curly hair, bright smiling eyes, and a strong arm, who was ready to strike down all ambition, divine or human, which raised its haughty head and dreamt of absolute dominion. The bow and the triangular arrow were his inseparable companions. Hayk was a true lover of independence. He it was, who, like Moses of old, led his people from the post-diluvian tyranny of Bel (Nimrod) in the plain of Shinar to the cold but free mountains of Armenia where he subjugated the native population (1). Bel at first plied him with messages of fair promise if he would return. But thc hero met them with a proud

68

and defiant answer. Soon after as was expected, Cadmus, the grandson of Hayk, brought tidings of an invasion of Armenia by the innumerable forces of Bel. Hayk marched south with his small but brave army to meet the tyrant on the shores of the sea (of Van) "whose briny waters teem with tiny fish" (2). Here began the battle. Hayk arranged his warriors in a triangle on a plateau among mountains in the presence of the great multitude of invaders. The first shock was so terrible and costly in men that Bel, confused and frightened, began to withdraw. But Hayk's unerring triangular arrow, piercing his breast, issued forth from his back. The overthrow of their chief was a signal for the mighty Babylonian forces to disperse.

Hayk is the eponymous hero of the Armenians according to their national name, Hay, used among themselves. From the same name they have called their country *Hayastan* or the Kingdom (Ashkharh = Iran. *Khshathra*) of the Hays. Adjectives derived from *Hayk* describe both gigantic strength and great beauty. Gregory of Narek calls even the beauty of the Holy Virgin, Hayk-like! The word Hayk itself was often used in the sense of a "giant."

Some have tried to give an astronomical interpretation to this legend. Pointing out the fact that Hayk is also the Armenian name for the constellation Orion, they have maintained that the triangular arrangement of Hayk's army reflects the triangle which the star Adaher in Orion forms with the two dogstars. However, any attempt to establish a parallelism between the Giant Orion and Hayk as we know him, is doomed to failure, for beyond a few minor or general points of resemblance, the two heroes have nothing in common. Hayk seems to have been also the older Armenian name of the Zodiacal sign Libra, and of the planet Mars (3), while the cycle of Sirius was for the Armenians the cycle of Hayk.

The best explanation of Hayk's name and history seems to lie in the probable identity of Hayk (Hayik, "little Hay," just as Armenak means "little Armenius") with the Phrygian sky-god Hyas whom the Greeks called *ues*. Both the Greeks and the Assyrians (4) know him as an independent Thraco-Phrygian deity. The Assyrians call him the god of Moschi (5). In a period when everything Thracian and Phrygian was being assimilated by Dionysos or was sinking into insignificance before his triumphant march through the Thraco-Phrygian world, Hyas, from a tribal deity, became an epithet of this god of vegetation and of wine. For us Hyas is no one else but the Vayu of the Vedas and the Avesta. So in the legend of Hayk we probably have the story of the battle between an Indo-European weather-god and the Mesopotamian Bel. It is very much more natural to derive a national name like Hay from a national deity's name, according to the well-known analogies of Assur and Khaldi, than to interpret it as *pati*,"chief" (6).

2. Armenak

According to Moses of Chorene, Armenak is the name of the son of Hayk. He chose for his abode the mountain Aragads (now Alagez) and the adjacent country.

He is undoubtedly another eponymous hero of the Armenian race. Armenius, father of Er, mentioned by Plato in his *Republic* (7), can be no other than this Armenak who, according to Moses of Chorene and the so-called Sebeos fragments, is the great-grandfather of Ara (Er). The final syllable is a diminutive, just as is the "k" in Hayk. Popular legend, which occupied itself a good deal with Hayk, seems to have neglected Armenak almost completely. It is quite possible that Armenak is the same as the Teutonic Irmin and the Vedic Aryaman, therefore originally a title of the sky-god. The many exploits ascribed to Aram, the father of Ara, may indeed, belong by right to Armenak (8).

3. Shara

Shara is said to be the son of Armais. As he was uncommonly voracious his father gave him the rich land of Shirak to prey upon. He was also far-famed for his numerous progeny. The old Armenian proverb used to say to gluttons: "If thou hast the throat (appetite) of Shara, we have not the granaries of Shirak."

One may suspect that an ogre is hiding behind this ancient figure. At all events his name must have some affinity with the Arabic word Sharah, which means gluttony (9).

4. Aram

Aram, a son of Harma, seems to be a duplicate of Armenak, although many scholars have identified him with Arame, a later king of Urartu, and with Aram, an eponymous hero of the Aramaic region. The Armenian national tradition makes him a conqueror of Barsham "whom the Syrians deified on account of his exploits," of a certain Nychar Mades (Nychar the Median), and of Paiapis Chalia, a Titan who ruled from the Pontus Euxinus to the Ocean (Mediterranean). Through this last victory Aram became the ruler of Pontus and Cappadocia upon which he imposed the Armenian language.

In this somewhat meagre and confused tale we have probably an Armenian god Aram or Armenius in war against the Syrian god Ba'al Shamin, some Median god or hero called Nychar (10), and a western Titan called Paiapis Chalia, who no doubt represents in a corrupt form the Urartian deity Khaldi with the Phrygian (?) title of Papaios. The legend about the Pontic war probably originated in the desire to explain how Armenians came to be found in Lesser Armenia, or it may be a distant and distorted echo of the Phrygo-Armenian struggles against the Hittite kingdoms of Asia Minor.

5. Ara, the Beautiful

With Ara we are unmistakably on mythological ground. Unfortunately this interesting hero has, like Hayk and Aram, greatly suffered at the hands of our ancient Hellenizers. The present form of the myth, a quasi-classical version of the original, is as follows: When Ninus, King of Assyria, died or fled to Crete from his wicked and voluptuous queen Semiramis, the latter having heard of the manly beauty of Ara, proposed to marry him or to hold him for a while as her lover. But Ara scornfully rejected her advances for the sake of his beloved wife Nvard. Incensed by this unexpected rebuff, the impetuous Semiramis came against Ara with a large force, not so much to punish him for his obstinacy as to capture him alive. Ara's army was routed and he fell dead during the bloody encounter. At the end of the day, his lifeless body having been found among the slain, Semiramis removed it to an upper room of his palace hoping that her gods (the dog-spirits called *Aralezes*) would restore him to life by licking his wounds. Although, according to the rationalizing Moses of Chorene, Ara did not rise from the dead, the circumstances which he mentions leave no doubt that the original myth made him come back to life and continue his rule over the Armenians in peace. For, according to this author (11), when Ara's body began to decay, Semiramis dressed up one of her lovers as Ara and pretended that the gods had fulfilled her wishes. She also erected a statue to the gods in thankfulness for this favor and pacified Armenian minds by persuading them that Ara was alive.

Another version of the Ara story is to be found at the end of Plato's *Republic* (12) where he tells us that a certain Pamphylian hero called Er, son of Armenius, "happening on a time to die in battle, when the dead were on the tenth day carried off, already corrupted, was taken up sound; and being carried home as he was about to be laid on the funeral pile, he revived, and being revived, he told what he saw of the other state." The long eschatological dissertation which follows is probably Thracian or Phrygian, as these peoples were especially noted for their speculations about the future life.

The Pamphylian Er's parentage, as well as the Armenian version of the same story, taken together, make it highly probable that we have here an Armenian (or Phrygian), rather than Pamphylian (13), myth, although by some queer chance it may have reached Greece from a Pamphylian source. Semiramis may be a popular or learned addition to the myth. But it is quite reasonable to assume that the original story represented the battle as caused by a disappointed woman or goddess. An essential element, preserved by Plato, is the report about life beyond the grave. The Armenian version reminds us strongly of that part of the Gilgamesh epic in which Ishtar appears in the forest of Cedars guarded by Khumbaba to allure Gilgamesh, a hero or demi-god, with attributes of a sun-god, into the role of Tammuz. We know how Gilgamesh refused her advances. Eabani, the companion of Gilgamesh, seems to be a first (primaeval) man who was turning his rugged face towards civilization through the love of a woman. He takes part in the wanderings of Gilgamesh, and fights with him against Ishtar and the heavenly bull sent by Anu to avenge the insulted goddess. Apparently wounded in this struggle Eabani dies. Thereupon Gilgamesh wanders to the world of the dead in search of the plant of life. On his return he meets with Eabani who has come back from the region of the dead to inform him of the condition of the departed and of the care with which the dead must be buried in order to make life in Aralu (Hades) bearable (14).

Possibly the original Ara story goes back to this Babylonian epic but fuses Gilgamesh and Eabani into one hero. Sayce suggests that Ara may be the Eri of the Vannic inscriptions and the latter may have been a sun-god (15).

6. Tigranes, the Dragon-Fighter

This story also must be interpreted mythologically, although it is connected with two historical characters. It is a dragon legend which does not contain the slightest fraction of historical fact, but was manifestly adapted to the story of Astyages in the first book of Herodotus. For the sake of brevity we shall not analyse it in detail, as its chief elements will be brought out in the chapter on dragons. The rationalizing zeal of the later Armenian authors has evidently made use of the fact that *Azhdahak*, "dragon,"was also the name of a famous Median king in the times of Cyrus the Great (16).

The legend was as follows: Tigranes (from *Tigrish*,"arrow," the old Iranian name of the Babylonian Nabu), King of Armenia, was a friend of Cyrus the Great. His immediate neighbor on the east, Azhdahak of Media, was in great fear of both these young rulers. One night in a dream, he saw himself in a strange land

73

near a lofty ice-clad mountain (the Massis). A tall, fair-eyed, red-cheeked woman, clothed in purple and wrapped in an azure veil was sitting on the summit of the higher peak, caught with the pains of travail. Suddenly she gave birth to three full-grown sons, one of whom, bridling a lion, rode westward. The second sat on a zebra and rode northward. But the third one, bridling a dragon, marched against Azhdahak of Media and made an onslaught on the idols to which the old king (the dreamer himself) was offering sacrifice and incense. There ensued between the Armenian knight and Astyages a bloody fight with spears, which ended in the overthrow of Azhdahak. In the morning, warned by his Magi of a grave and imminent danger from Tigranes, Azhdahak decides to marry Tigranuhi, the sister of Tigranes, in order to use her as an instrument in the destruction of her brother. His plan succeeds up to the point of disclosing his intentions to Tigranuhi. Alarmed by these she immediately puts her brother on his guard. Thereupon the indomitable Tigranes brings about an encounter with Azhdahak in which he plunges his triangular spear-head into the tyrant's bosom pulling out with it a part of his lungs (17). Tigranuhi had already managed to come to her brother even before the battle. After this signal victory, Tigranes compels Azhdahak's family to move to Armenia and settle around Massis. These are the children of the dragon, says the inveterate rationalizer, about whom the old songs tell fanciful stories, and Anush, the mother of dragons, is no one but the first queen of Azhdahak (18).

Fig. 3. Bronze Figures

Found in Van usually explained as Semiramis in the form of a dove and possibly representing the Goddess Sharis, the Urartian Ishtar.

Footnotes

1. Here, of course, the valuable tale of the epics has vanished before blical conception of the spread of mankind, but a dim memory of the events that led to the separation of the Armenians from their mighty brethren of Thrace or Phrygia, as well as something of the story of the conquest of Urartu by the Armenians, seems to be reflected in the biblicised form of the legend.

2. Moses, i. 10, 11.

3. Alishan, p. 126.

4. Dr. Chapman calls my attention to the passages in Sayce's and Sandalgian's works on the Urartian inscriptions, where they find the name Huas or 'Uas. Sandalgian also explains it as Hayk. (*Inscriptions Cuneiformes Urartiques*, 1900, p. 437.) See also the fix on Vahagn in this work.

5. A. H. Sayce, *The Cuneiform Inscriptions of Van*, p. 719.

6. This is the prevailing view among modern scholars. The word that was current in this sense in historical times was *azat* (from *yazata?*), "venerable." Patrubani sees in Hayk the Sanskrit *pana* and the Vedic *payn*, "keeper"; Armen. *hay-im*, "I look."

7. Republic, x. 134.

8. Patrubani explains *Armenus* as *Arya-Manah*, "Aryan (noble?)-minded." The Vedic Aryaman seems to mean "friend," "comrade."

9. This is not impossible in itself as we find a host of Arabic words and even broken plurals in pre-Muhammedan Armenian.

10. Nychar is perhaps the Assyrian Nakru, "enemy "or a thinned-down and very corrupt echo of the name of Hanaçiruka of Mata, mentioned in an inscription of Shamshi-Rammon of Assyria, 825-812 B.C. (Harper, *Ass. and Bab. Liter.*, p. +8).

11. Moses, i. 15. See also additional note on Semiramis, Appendix III.

12. *Republic*, x. 134.

13. Pamphylians were dressed up like the Phrygians, but they were a mixed race.

14. See art. "Gilgamesh" in EBr 11; also F. Jeremiah's account of the myth in Chantepie de la Saussaye, *Lehrbuch*, i. 331 f. Frazer in GB part iv, *Adonis, Attis and Osiris*, ch. 5, gives an interesting account of kings, who, through self-cremation on a funeral pyre, sought to become deified. He tells also of a person who, having died, was brought back to life through the plant of life shown by a serpent (as in the well-known myth of Polyidus and Glaucus, cf. Hyginus, *Fab.* 136, and for Folk-tale

parallels, J. Bolte and G. Polivka, *Anmerkungen zu den Kinder- und Haus-Marchen der Bruder Grimm*, Leipzig, 1913, i. 126 f.). Further, we learn through Herodotus (iv. 95.) that Zalmoxis, the Sabazios of the Getae in Thrace, taught about the life beyond the grave, and demonstrated his teaching by disappearing and appearing again.

15. Sayce, *Cuneiform Inscriptions of Van*, p. 566. We may also point to the verbal resemblance between Er-Ara and the Bavarian Er, which seems to have been either a title of Tiu = Dyaus, or the name of an ancient god corresponding to Tiu.

16. For the real Tigranes of this time we may refer the reader to Xenophon, *Cyropaedia*, iii. I. Azdahak of Media is known to Greek authors as Astyages, the maternal grandfather of Cyrus the Great.

17. According to classical authors the historical Astyages was not killed by Tigranes, but dethroned and taken captive by Cyrus.

18. According to Herodotus (i. 74) the name of the first queen of Astyages was Aryenis. *Anush* is a Persian word which may be interpreted as "pleasant." But it may also be a shortened form from *anushiya*, "devoted." This latter sense is supported by such compound names in Armenian as connect *anush* with names of gods, e.g. Haykanush, Hranush, Vartanush, etc.

Chapter XI

The World of Spirits and Monsters

THE ARMENIAN world of spirits and monsters teems with elements both native and foreign. Most of the names are of Persian origin, although we do not know how much of this lore came directly from Iran. For we may safely assert that the majority of these uncanny beings bear a general Indo-European, one might even say, universal character. So any attempt to explain them locally, as dim memories of ancient monsters or of conquered and exterminated races will in the long run prove futile. One marked feature of this vital and ever-living branch of mythology is the world-wide uniformity of the fundamental elements. Names, places, forms, combinations may come and go, but the beliefs which underlie the varying versions of the stories remain rigidly constant. On this ground mythology and folklore join hands.

The chief actors in this lower, but very deeply rooted stratum of religion and mythology are serpents and dragons, good or evil ghosts and fairies, among whom we should include the nymphs of the classical world, the elves and kobolds of the Teutons, the *vilas* of the Slavs, the *jinn* and *dev*s of Islam, etc. (1).

At this undeveloped stage of comparative folklore it would be rash to posit a common origin for all these multitudinous beings. Yet they show, in their feats and characteristics, many noteworthy interrelations and similarities all over the world.

Leaving aside the difficult question whether serpent-worship precedes and underlies all other religion and mythology, we have cumulative evidence, both ancient and modern, of a world-wide belief that the serpent stands in the closest relation to the ghost. The genii, the ancestral spirits, usually appear in the form of a serpent. As serpents they reside in and protect, their old homes. Both the serpent and the ancestral ghost have an interest in the fecundity of the family and the fertility of the fields. They possess superior wisdom, healing power, and dispose of wealth, etc. They do good to those whom they love, harm to those whom they hate. Then these serpents and dragons frequently appear as the physical manifestation of other spirits than ghosts, and so we have a large class of serpent-fairies in all ages and in many parts of the world, like the serpent mother of the Scythian race (2), and like Melusine, the serpent-wife of Count Raymond of Poitiers (Lusignan). Further, the ghosts, especially the evil ones, have a great affinity with demons. Like demons they harass men, with sickness and other disasters. In fact, in the minds of many people, they pass over entirely into the ranks of the demons.

Keeping, then, in mind the fact that, as far back and as far out as our knowledge can reach, the peoples of the world have established sharp distinctions between these various creatures of superstitious imagination, let us run over some of the feats and traits which are ascribed to all or most of them. This will serve as an appropriate introduction to the ancient Armenian material.

They all haunt houses as protectors or persecutors; live in ruins, not because these are ruins, but because they are ancient sites; have a liking for difficult haunts like mountains, caves, ravines, forests, stony places; live and roam freely in bodies of water, such as springs, wells, rivers, lakes, seas; possess subterranean palaces, realms and gardens, and dispose of hidden treasures; although they usually externalize themselves as serpents, they have a marked liking for the human shape, in which they often appear. They exhibit human habits, needs, appetites, passions, and organizations. Thus they are born, grow, and die (at least by a violent death). They are hungry and thirsty and have a universal weakness for milk; they often steal grain and go a-hunting. They love and hate, marry and give in marriage. In this, they often prefer the fair sons and daughters of men (especially noble-born ladies), with whom they come to live or whom they carry off to their subterranean abodes. The result of these unions is often—not always—a weird, remarkable, sometimes also very wicked, progeny. They steal human children, leaving changelings in their stead. They usually (but not always) appear about midnight and disappear before the dawn, which is heralded by cockcrow. They cause insanity by entering the human body. Flint, iron, fire, and lightning, and sometimes also water (3) are very repugnant to them. They hold the key to magical lore, and in all things have a superior knowledge, usually combined with a very strange credulity. They may claim worship and often sacrifices, animal as well as human.

Although these beings may be classified as corporeal and incorporeal, and even one species may, at least in certain countries, have a corporeal as well as incorporeal variety, it is safe to assert that their corporeality itself is usually of a subtle, airy kind and that the psychical aspect of their being is by far the predominating one. This is true even of the serpent and the dragon. Finally, in one way or another, all of these mysterious or monstrous beings have affinities with chthonic powers.

Largely owing to such common traits running through almost the whole of the material, it is difficult to subject the Armenian data to a clean-cut classification.

1. The Shahapet of Localities

The Shahapet (Iranian *Khshathrapati*, Zd. *Shoithrapaiti*, lord of the field or of the land) is nothing else than the very widely known serpent-ghost (genius) of places, such as fields, woods, mountains, houses, and, especially, graveyards. It appears both as man and as serpent. In connection with houses, the Armenian Shahapet was probably some ancestral ghost which appeared usually as a serpent. Its character was always good except when angered. According to the Armenian translation of John Chrysostom, even the vinestocks and the olive-trees had Shahapets. In Agathangelos Christ Himself was called the

Shahapet of graveyards (4), evidently to contradict or correct a strong belief in the serpent-keeper of the resting place of the dead. We know that, in Hellenistic countries, gravestones once bore the image of serpents. We have no classical testimony to the Shahapet of homesteads, but modern Armenian folklore, and especially the corrupt forms Shvaz and Shvod, show that the old Shahapet of Armenia was both a keeper of the fields and a keeper of the house. The Shvaz watches over the agricultural products and labours, and appears to men once a year in the spring. The Shvod is a guardian of the house. Even today people scare naughty little children with his name. But the identity of these two is established by a household ceremony which is of far-off kinship to the Roman *paternalia*, itself an old festival of the dead or of ghosts, which was celebrated from February 13 to 21. In this connection Miss Harrison has some remarks "on the reason for the placating of ghosts when the activities of agriculture were about to begin and the powers of the underground world were needed to stimulate fertility" (5). But the Armenians did not placate them with humble worship and offerings: they rather forced them to go to the fields and take part in the agricultural labours. This ancient ceremony in its present form may be described as follows (6): On the last day of February the Armenian peasants, armed with sticks, bags, old clothes, etc., strike the walls of the houses and barns saying: "Out with the Shvod and in with March!" On the previous night a dish of water was placed on the threshold, because, as we have seen, water is supposed to help the departure of the spirits, an idea also underlying the use of water by the Slavic peoples in their burial rites. Therefore, as soon as the dish is overturned, they close the doors tightly and make the sign of the cross. Evidently, this very old and quaint rite aims at driving the household spirits to the fields, and the pouring out of the water is regarded as a sign of their departure. According to the description in the Pshrank, the Shvods, who are loath to part with their winter comforts, have been seen crying and asking, "What have we done to be driven away in this fashion?" Also they take away clean garments with them and return them soon in a soiled condition, no doubt as a sign of their hard labours in the fields.

The house-serpent brings good luck to the house, and

sometimes also gold. So it must be treated very kindly and respectfully. If it departs in anger, there will be in that house endless trouble and privation. Sometimes they appear in the middle of the night as strangers seeking hospitality and it pays to be kind and considerate to them, as otherwise they may depart in anger, leaving behind nothing but sorrow and misfortune.

As there are communal hearths, so there are also district serpents. The serpent-guardian of a district discriminates carefully between strangers and the inhabitants of the district, hurting the former but leaving the latter in peace (7).

As the Armenian ghost differs little from other ghosts in its manner of acting, we shall refer the reader for a fuller description to the minute account of it given in Abeghian's *Armenischer Volksglaube* (chapters 2 and 6).

2. Dragons

The close kinship of the dragon with the serpent has always been recognized. Not only have they usually been thought to be somewhat alike in shape, but they have also many mythical traits in common, such as the dragon's blood, the serpent's or the dragon's stone (8), the serpent's or the dragon's egg, both of the latter being talismans of great value with which we meet all over the world and in all times. They are corporeal beings, but they have a certain amount of the ghostly and the demoniac in them. Both can be wicked, but in folklore and mythology they are seldom as thoroughly so as in theology. Of the two, the dragon is the more monstrous and demoniac in character, especially associated in the people's minds (9) with evil spirits. He could enter the human body and possess it, causing the victim to whistle. But even he had redeeming qualities, on account of which his name could be adopted by kings and his emblem could wave over armies. In the popular belief of Iran the dragon can not have been such a hopeless reprobate as he appears in the Avestan Azhi Dahaka.

Mount Massis, wrongly called Ararat by Europeans, was the main home of the Armenian dragon. The volcanic character of this lofty peak, with its earthquakes, its black smoke and lurid flames in time of eruption, may have suggested its association with that dread monster. But the mountain was sacred independently of dragons, and it was called Azat (i.e., *Yazata* (?), "venerable").

The Armenian for dragon is Vishap, a word of Persian origin meaning "with poisonous saliva." It was an adjective that once qualified Azhi Dahaka, but attained an independent existence even in Iran. In the Armenian myths one may plausibly distinguish "the chief dragon" and the dragons, although these would be bound together by family ties; for the dragon breeds and multiplies its kind. The old songs told many a wonderful and mysterious tale about the dragon and the brood or children of the dragon that lived around the Massis. Most of these stories have a close affinity with western fairy tales. Some wicked dragon had carried away a fair princess called Tigranuhi, seemingly with her own consent. Her brother, King Tigranes, a legendary character, slew the dragon with his spear in a single combat and delivered the abducted maiden (10).

Queen Sathenik, the Albanian wife of King Artaxias, fair and fickle as she was, had been bewitched into a love affair with a certain Argavan who was a chief in the tribe of the dragons. Argavan induced Artaxias himself to partake of a banquet given in his honour in "the palace of the dragons," where he attempted some treacherous deed against his royal guest. The nature of the plot is not stated, but the King must have escaped with his life for he kept his faithless queen and died a natural death (11).

The dragon (or the children of the dragons) used to steal children and put in their stead a little evil spirit of their own brood, who was always wicked of character. An outstanding victim of this inveterate habit—common to the dragons and Devs of Armenia and their European cousins, the fairies (12)—was Artavasd, son of the above mentioned Artaxias, the friend of Hannibal in exile and the builder of Artaxata. History tells us that Artavasd, during his short life, was perfectly true to the type of his uncanny ancestry, and when he suddenly disappeared by falling down a precipice of the venerable Massis, it was reported that spirits of the mountain or the dragons themselves had caught him up and carried him off.

More important than all these tales, Vahagn, the Armenian god of fire (lightning), won the title of "dragon-reaper" by fighting against dragons like Indra of old. Although the details of these encounters have not come down to us, the dragons in them must have been allied to Vrtra, the spirit of drought.

The epic songs mentioned also Anush, as the wife of the dragon and the mother of the children of the dragon. She lived in the famous ravine in the higher peak of the Massis.

The records as they stand, permit us to conjecture that besides the dragon as such, there was also a race of dragon-men, born of the intermarriage of the dragon with human wives. But we cannot be very certain of this, although there would be nothing strange in it, as the history of human beliefs teems with the "serpent fathers" of remarkable men, and the character of the Iranian Azhi Dahaka himself easily lends itself to these things. The children of the dragon also, whether mixed beings or not, dwelt around the Massis and were regarded as uncanny people with a strong bent towards, and much skill in, witchcraft (13).

However it may be about the children of the dragon, it is incontestable that the dragons themselves were a very real terror for the ancient Armenians. We are told that they lived in a wide ravine left by an earthquake on the side of the higher peak of the Massis. According to Moses, Eznik, and Vahram Vardapet (14), they had houses and palaces on high mountains, in one of which, situated on the Massis, King Artaxias had enjoyed the dangerous banquet we have mentioned.

These dragons were both corporeal and personal beings with a good supply of keen intelligence and magical power. They boasted a gigantic size and a terrible voice (Eghishe). But the people were neither clear nor unanimous about their real shape. They were usually imagined as great serpents and as sea-monsters, and such enormous beasts of the land or sea were called dragons, perhaps figuratively. We find no allusion to their wings, but Eznik says that the Lord pulls the dragon up "through so-called oxen" in order to save men from his poisonous breath (15). The dragons appeared in any form they chose, but preferably as men and as serpents, like the *jinn* of the Arabs. They played antics to obtain their livelihood. They loved to suck the milk of the finest cows (16). With their beasts of burden or in the guise of mules and camels they were wont to carry away the best products of the soil. So the keepers of the threshing floor, after the harvest, often shouted, "Hold fast! Hold fast!" (*Kal! Kal!*) probably to induce them to leave the grain by treating them as guarding genii (17). But they carefully avoided saying "Take! Take!" (*Ar! Ar!*).

The dragons also went hunting just as did the Kaches with whom we shall presently meet. They were sometimes seen running in pursuit of the game (Vahram Vardapet) and they laid traps or nets in the fields for birds. All these things point to the belief that their fashion of living was like that of men in a primitive stage of development, a trait which we find also in western and especially Celtic fairies.

It would seem that the dragons as well as their incorporeal cousins the Kaches claimed and kept under custody those mortals who had originally belonged to their stock. Thus Artavasd was bound and held captive in a cave of the Massis for fear that he might break loose and dominate or destroy the world (18). Alexander the Great, whose parentage from a serpent or dragon-father was a favorite theme of the eastern story-mongers, was, according to the medieval Armenians, confined by the dragons in a bottle and kept in their mountain palace at Rome. King Erwand also, whose name, according to Alishan, means serpent, was held captive by the dragons in rivers and mist. He must have been a changeling, or rather born of a serpent-father. For he was a worshipper of Devs and, according to Moses, the son of a royal princess from an unknown father. He was proverbially ugly and wicked and possessed an evil eye under the gaze of which rocks crumbled to pieces (19).

Like most peoples of the world, Armenians have always

85

associated violent meteorological phenomena with the dragon. This association was very strong in their mind. In a curious passage in which Eghishe (fifth century) compares the wrath of Yezdigerd I to a storm, the dragon is in the very centre of the picture. We need not doubt that this dragon was related to the foregoing, although ancient testimony on this subject leaves much to be desired. Eznik's account of the ascension of the dragon " through so-called oxen " into the sky, is in perfect accord with the mediaeval Armenian accounts of the " pulling up of the dragon." This process was always accompanied by thunder, lightning, and heavy showers. Vanakan Vardapet says: "They assert that the Vishap (the dragon) is being pulled up. The winds blow from different directions and meet each other. This is a whirlwind. If they do not overcome each other, they whirl round each other and go upward. The fools who see this, imagine it to be the dragon or something else" (20). Another mediaeval author says: "The whirlwind is a wind that goes upward. Wherever there are abysses or crevasses in the earth, the wind has entered the veins of the earth and then having found an opening, rushes up together in a condensed cloud with a great tumult, uprooting the pine-trees, snatching away rocks and lifting them up noisily to drop them down again. This is what they call pulling up the dragon" (21).

Whether the dragon was merely a personification of the whirlwind, the water spout, and the storm cloud is a hard question which we are not ready to meet with an affirmative answer, like Abeghian (22) who follows in this an older school. Such a simple explanation tries to cover too many diverse phenomena at once and forgets the fundamental fact that the untutored mind of man sees many spirits at work in nature, but rarely, if ever, personifies Nature itself. To him those spirits are very real, numerous, somewhat impersonal and versatile, playing antics now on the earth, now in the skies, and now under the ground. In the case of the dragon causing storms, to the Armenian mind the storm seems to be a secondary concomitant of the lifting up of the dragon which threatens to destroy the earth (23). Yet, that the original, or at least the most outstanding dragon-fight was one between the thunder or lightning-god and the dragon that withholds the waters is an important point which must not be lost sight of (24).

We must not forget to mention the worship that the dragon enjoyed. Eznik says that Satan, making the dragon appear appallingly large, constrained men to worship him. This worship was no doubt similar in character to the veneration paid to evil spirits in many lands and perhaps not entirely distinguished from serpent-worship. According to the same writer, at least in Sassanian times even Zrvantists (magians?) indulged in a triennial worship of the devil on the ground that he is evil by will not by nature, and that he may do good or even be converted (25). But there was nothing regular or prescribed about this act, which was simply dictated by fear. As the black hen and the black cock (26) make their appearance often in general as well as Armenian folk-lore as an acceptable sacrifice to evil spirits, we may reasonably suppose that they had some role in the marks of veneration paid to the dragon in ancient times. But we have also more definite testimony in early martyrological writing (*History of St. Hripsimeans*) about dragon worship. The author, after speaking of the cult of fire and water (above quoted) adds: "And two dragons, devilish and black, had fixed their dwelling in the cave of the rock, to which young virgins and innocent youths were sacrificed. The devils, gladdened by these sacrifices and altars, by the sacred fire and spring, produced a wonderful sight with flashes, shakings and leapings. And the deep valley (below) was full of venomous snakes and scorpions."

Finally the myth about the dragon's blood was also known to the Armenians. The so-called "treaty" between Constantine and Tiridates, which is an old but spurious document, says that Constantine presented his Armenian ally with a spear which had been dipped in the dragon's blood. King Arshag, son of Valarshag, also had a spear dipped in the blood of "reptiles" with which he could pierce thick stones (27). Such arms were supposed to inflict incurable wounds.

3. Kaches

The Kaches form a natural link between the Armenian dragon and the Armenian Devs of the present day. In fact they are probably identical with the popular (not theological) Devs. They are nothing more or less than the European fairies, kobolds, etc. Their name means "the brave ones," which is an old euphemism (like the present day Armenian expression "our betters," or like the Scots "gude folk") used of the spirit world and designed to placate powerful, irresponsible beings of whose intentions one could never be sure. From the following statements of their habits and feats one may clearly see how the people connected or confused them with the dragons. Our sources are the ancient and mediaeval writers. Unlike the dragon the Kaches were apparently incorporeal beings, spirits, good in themselves, according to the learned David the Philosopher, but often used by God to execute penalties. Like the Devs, they lingered preferably in stony places with which they were usually associated and Mount Massis was one of their favorite haunts. Yet they could be found almost everywhere. The country was full of localities bearing their name and betraying their presence, like the Stone of the Kaches, the Town of the Kaches, the Village of the Kaches, the Field of the Kaches (*Katchavar*) "where the Kaches coursed ", etc.(28).

Like the dragons, they had palaces on high sites. According to an old song it was these spirits who carried the wicked Artavazd up the Massis, where he still remains an impatient prisoner. They hold also Alexander the Great in Rome, and King Erwand in rivers and darkness, i.e., mists (29). They waged wars, which is a frequent feature of serpent and fairy communities, and they went hunting (30). They stole the grain from the threshing floor and the wine from the wine press. They often found pleasure in beating, dragging, torturing men, just as their brothers and sisters in the West used to pinch their victims black and blue. Men were driven out of their wits through their baleful influence. Votaries of the magical art in medieval Armenia were wont, somewhat like Faust and his numerous tribe, to gallop off, astride of big earthen jars (31), to far-off places, and walking on water, they arrived in foreign countries where they laid tables before the gluttonous Kaches and received instructions from them. Last of all, the mediaeval Kaches (and probably also their ancestors) were very musical. The people often heard their singing, although we do not know whether their performance was so enthralling as that ascribed to the fairies in the West and to the Greek sirens. However, their modern representatives seem to prefer human music to their own. According to Djvanshir, a historian of the Iberians of Transcaucasia, the wicked Armenian King Erwand built a temple to the Kaches at Dsung, near Akhalkaghak in Iberia (Georgia).

4. Javerzaharses (Nymphs)

These are not mentioned in the older writers, so it is not quite clear whether they are a later importation from other countries or not. They probably are female Kaches, and folklore knows the latter as their husbands. Alishan, without quoting any authority, says that they wandered in prairies, among pines, and on the banks of rivers. They were invisible beings, endowed with a certain unacquired and imperishable knowledge. They could neither learn anything new nor forget what they knew. They had rational minds which were incapable of development. They loved weddings, singing, tambourines, and rejoicings, so much so, that some of the later ecclesiastical writers confused them as a kind of evil spirits against whose power of temptation divine help must be invoked. In spite of their name ("perpetual brides") they were held to be mortal (32). The common people believed that these spirits were especially interested in the welfare, toilette, marriage, and childbirth of maidens. There are those who have supposed that Moses of Chorene was thinking of these charming spirits when he wrote the following cryptic words : "The rivers having quietly gathered on their borders along the knees (?) of the mountains and the fringes of the fields, the youths wandered as though at the side of maidens."

5. Torch (or Torx)

Torch is in name and character related to the Duergar (Zwerge, dwarfs) of Northern Europe and to the Telchins of Greece or rather of Rhodes (33). This family of strange names belongs evidently to the Indo-European language, and designated a class of demons of gigantic or dwarfish size, which were believed to possess great skill in all manner of arts and crafts. They were especially famous as blacksmiths. In antiquity several mythical works were ascribed to the Greek Telchins, such as the scythe of Cronos and the trident of Poseidon. They were mischievous, spiteful genii who from time immemorial became somewhat confused with the Cyclops. The Telchins were called children of the sea and were found only in a small number .

The Torch, who can hardly be said to be a later importation from Greece, and probably belongs to a genuine Phrygo-Armenian myth, resembles both the Telchins and the Cyclops. In fact he is a kind of Armenian Polyphemos. He was said to be of the race of Pascham (?) and boasted an ugly face, a gigantic and coarse frame, a flat nose, and deep-sunk and cruel eyes. His home was sought in the west of Armenia most probably in the neighbourhood of the Black Sea. The old epic songs could not extol enough his great physical power and his daring. The feats ascribed to him were more wonderful than those of Samson, Herakles, or even Rustem Sakjik (of Segistan), whose strength was equal to that of one hundred and twenty elephants (34).

With his bare hands the Armenian Torch could crush a solid piece of hard granite. He could smooth it down into a slab and engrave upon it pictures of eagles and other objects with his finger-nails. He was, therefore, known as a great artisan and even artist.

Once he met with his foes, on the shores of the Black Sea, when he was sore angered by something which they had evidently done to him. At his appearance they took to the sea and succeeded in laying eight leagues between themselves and the terrible giant. But he, nothing daunted by this distance, began to hurl rocks as large as hills at them. Several of the ships were engulfed in the abyss made by these crude projectiles and others were driven off many leagues by the mighty waves the rocks had started rolling (35).

6. The Devs

Ahriman, the chief of the Devs, was known in Armenia only as a Zoroastrian figure. The Armenians themselves probably called their ruler of the powers of evil, *Char*, "the evil one." Just as Zoroastrianism recognized *zemeka*, "winter," as an arch demon, so the Armenians regarded snow, ice, hail, storms, lightning, darkness, dragons and other beasts, as the creatures of the *Char* or the Devs (36). Although they knew little of a rigid dualism in the moral world or of a constant warfare between the powers of light and the powers of darkness, they had, besides all the spirits that we have described and others with whom we have not yet met, a very large number of Devs. These are called also *ais* (a cognate of the Sanscrit *asu* and Teutonic *as* or *aes*), which Eznik explains as "breath." Therefore a good part of the Devs were pictured as beings of "air." They had, like the Mohammedan angels, a subtile body. They were male and female, and lived in marital relations not only with each other, but often also with human beings (37). They were born and perhaps died. Nor did they live in a state of irresponsible anarchy, but they were, so to speak, organized under the absolute rule of a monarch. In dreams they often assumed the form of wild beasts (38) in order to frighten men. But they appeared also in waking hours both as human beings and as serpents (39).

Stony places, no doubt also ruins, were their favorite haunts, and from such the most daring men would shrink. Once when an Armenian noble was challenging a Persian viceroy of royal blood to ride forward on a stony ground, the Prince retorted: "Go thou forward, seeing that the Devs alone can course in stony places." (40)

Yet according to a later magical text, there can be nothing in which a Dev may not reside and work. Swoons and insanity, yawning and stretching, sneezing, and itching around the throat or ear or on the tongue, were unmistakable signs of their detested presence. But men were not entirely helpless against the Devs. Whoever would frequently cut the air or strike suspicious spots with a stick or sword, or even keep these terrible weapons near him while sleeping, could feel quite secure from their endless molestations (41). Of course, we must distinguish between the popular Dev, who is a comparatively foolish and often harmless giant, and the theological Dev, who is a pernicious and ever harmful spirit laying snares on the path of man. To the latter belonged, no doubt, the Druzhes (the Avestic Drujes), perfidious, lying, and lewd female spirits. Their Avestic mode of self-propagation, by tempting men in their dreams (42), is not entirely unknown to the Armenians. They probably formed a class by themselves like the Pariks (43). (Zoroastrian *Pairikas*, enchantresses), who also were pernicious female spirits, although the common people did not quite know whether they were Devs or monsters (44). These, too, were mostly to be sought and found in ruins (45).

7. Als

The most gruesome tribe of this demoniac world was that of the Als. It came to the Armenians either through the Syrians or through the Persians, who also believe in them and hold them to be demons of child-birth (46). Al is the Babylonian *Alu*, one of the four general names for evil spirits. But the Armenian and Persian Al corresponds somewhat to the Jewish Lilith and Greek Lamia.

Probably the Als were known to the ancient Armenians, but it is a noteworthy fact that we do not hear about them until medieval times. They appear as half-animal and half-human beings, shaggy and bristly. They are male and female and have a "mother" (47). They were often called beasts, nevertheless they were usually mentioned with Devs and Kaches. According to Gregory of Datev (48) they lived in watery, damp and sandy places, but they did not despise corners in houses and stables. A prayer against the Als describes them as impure spirits with fiery eyes, holding a pair of iron scissors in their hands, wandering or sitting in sandy places. Another unnamed author describes an Al as a man sitting on the sand. He has snake-like hair, finger-nails of brass, teeth of iron and the tusk of a boar. They have a king living in abysses, whom they serve, and who

92

is chained and sprinkled up to the neck with (molten?) lead and shrieks continually.

The Als were formerly disease-demons who somehow came to restrict their baleful activities to unborn children and their mothers. They attack the latter in child-birth, scorching her ears, pulling out her liver and strangling her along with the unborn babe. They also steal unborn children of seven months, at which time these are supposed in the East to be fully formed and mature, in order to take them "deaf and dumb" (as a tribute?) to their dread king (49). In other passages they are said to blight and blind the unborn child, to suck its brain and blood, to eat its flesh, and to cause miscarriage, as well as to prevent the flow of the mother's milk. In all countries women in child-bed are thought to be greatly exposed to the influence and activity of evil spirits. Therefore, in Armenia, they are surrounded during travail with iron weapons and instruments with which the air of their room and the waters of some neighbouring brook (where these spirits are supposed to reside) are frequently beaten (50). If, after giving birth to the child, the mother faints, this is construed as a sign of the Al's presence. In such cases the people sometimes resort to an extreme means of saving the mother, which consists in exposing the child on a flat roof as a peace-offering to the evil spirits (51). Identical or at least very closely connected with the Al is Thepla, who by sitting upon a woman in child-bed causes the child to become black and faint and to die (52).

8. Nhangs

These monster spirits, at least in Armenian mythology, stand close to the dragons. The word means in Persian, "crocodile," and the language has usually held to this matter-of-fact sense, although in the Persian folk-tale of Hatim Tai, the Nhang appears in the semi-mythical character of a sea-monster, which is extremely large and which is afraid of the crab. The Armenian translators of the Bible use the word in the sense of "crocodile" and "hippopotamus." However, the Nhangs of Armenian mythology, which has confused an unfamiliar river monster with mythical beings, were personal (53) and incorporeal. They were evil spirits which had fixed their abode in certain places and assiduously applied themselves to working harm. They sometimes appeared as women (mermaids?) in the rivers. At other times they became seals (*phok*) and, catching the swimmer by the feet, dragged him to the bottom of the stream, where, perhaps, they had dwellings like the fairies (54). In a geography (still in MS.) ascribed to Moses, the Nhangs are said to have been observed in the river Aratsani (Murad Chay?) and in the Euphrates. After using an animal called *charchasham* for their lust, vampire-like they sucked its blood and left it dead. The same author reports that, according to some, the Nhang was a beast, and according to others, a Dev. John Chrysostom (in the Armenian translations) describes the daughter of Herodias as more bloodthirsty than "the Nhangs of the sea." (55)

9. Arlez (also Aralez, Jaralez)

Ancient Armenians believed that when a brave man fell in battle or by the hand of a treacherous foe, spirits called "Arlez" descended to restore him to life by licking his wounds. In the Ara myth, these spirits are called the gods of Semiramis; also in a true and realistic story of the fourth century about the murder of Mushegh Mamigonian, the commander of the Armenian king's forces (56) "His family could not believe in his death...others expected him to rise; so they sewed the head upon the body and they placed him upon a tower, saying, 'Because he was a brave man, the Arlez will descend and raise him.'" Presumably their name is Armenian, and means "lappers of brave men," or " lappers of Ara," (57) or even "ever-lappers." They were invisible spirits, but they were derived from dogs (58). No one ever saw them. Evidently the dogs from which they were supposed to have descended were ordinary dogs, with blood and flesh, for Eznik wonders how beings of.a higher spiritual order could be related to bodily creatures. The Arlez were imagined to exist in animal form as dogs (59).

10. Other Spirits and Chimeras

The Armenians believed also in the existence of chimeras by the name of *Hambari*s or *Hambaru*s, *Jushkaparik*s (*Vushkaparik*s), *Pai*s, and sea-bulls, all of which are manifestly of Persian provenience. Yet the nature and habits of these beings are hidden in confusion and mystery.

The Hambarus are born and die. They appear to men assuming perhaps different forms like the Devs and Pasviks. They are probably feminine beings with a body, living on land and particularly, in desert places or ruins. Von Stackelberg thinks that the word *Hambaruna* means in Persian, "house-spirits." This is possibly justified by the shorter form, *Anbar*, which may convey the sense of the falling of a house or wall; so the original Hambaru may be interpreted as a ghostly, inhabitant of a deserted place. The word may also mean "beautiful" or even "a hyena." An old Armenian dictionary defines it as *Charthogh* (?) if it lives on land, and as "crocodile," if it lives in water. But the oldest authorities, like the Armenian version of the Bible and Eznik, consider the Hambarus as mythological beings. Threatening Babylon with utter destruction Isaiah (Armenian version, xiii. 21-22) says, "There shall the wild beasts rest and their houses shall be filled with shrieks. There shall the Hambarus take their abode and the Devs shall dance there. The Jushkapariks shall dwell therein and the porcupines shall give birth to their little ones in their palaces." Hambaru here and elsewhere is used to render the *seiren* (siren) of the Septuagint (60).

Another chimerical being was the Jushkaparik or Vushkaparik, the Ass-Pairika, an indubitably Persian conception about which the Persian sources leave us in the lurch. Its name would indicate a half-demoniac and half-animal being, or a Pairika (a female Dev with amorous propensities) that appeared in the form of an ass and lived in ruins. However Eznik and the ancient translators of the Bible use the word through a hardly justifiable approximation to translate *Onokentauros*, the ass-bull of the Septuagint (Isaiah xiii. 22, xxxiv. I I, 14). According to Vahram Vardapet (quoted by Alishan) the Jushkaparik was imagined, in the middle ages, as a being that was half-man and half-ass, with a mouth of brass. Thus it came nearer the conception of a centaur, which word it served to translate in Moses of Khoren's history. Sometimes also to make the confusion more confounded, it is found in the sense of a siren and as a synonym of Hambaru.

We are completely in the dark in regard to the Pais which boasted human parenthood (presumably human mothers). There were those in Eznik's time who asserted that they had seen the Pais with their own eyes. The old Armenians spoke also of the Man-Pai (61). The Pais seem to be a variety of the Pariks.

The case is not so hopeless with the sea-bull, a chimerical monster which propagated its kind through the cow, somewhat after the manner of the sea-horses of Sinbad the Sailor's first voyage. Men asserted that in their village the sea-bull assaulted cows and that they often heard his roaring. We can well imagine that immediately after birth, the brood of the monster betook themselves to the water, like the sea-colts of the Arabian Nights' story which we have just mentioned (62). But this sea-bull may also recall the one which Poseidon sent to Minos for a sacrifice and which was by the wise king unwisely diverted from its original purpose and conveyed to his herds, or the one which, on the request of Theseus, Poseidon sent to destroy Theseus' innocent son, Hippolytus.

Another such chimeric monster, but surely not the last of the long list, was the elephant-goat (*phlachal*) (63).

Footnotes

1. See art. "Fairy" in ERE v. 678 f. See also Kirk, *Secret Com monwealth of Elves*, etc. Its analysis largely supports ours which was made independently on the basis of more extensive material.

2. Herodotus, iv. 9. The Greek view of the origin of the Scythians was that they were born from the union of Herakles with a woman who was human above the waist and serpent below.

3. Goldziher, "Wasser als Diimonenabruhrendes Mittel," in ARW, xiii. [1910] 274 f. This may have reference to water in its relation to the birth of fire or to the lightning.

4. Agathangelos, p. 57. Cf. the cross of the archangel Michael in graveyards of Roman Catholic churches, e.g., French.

5. *Prolegomena to the Study of Greek Religion*, Cambridge, 1903, p. 540.

6. This description is based on the account given by Alishan and in Pshrank. Some confusion has arisen in regard to the true nature of this old rite, owing to the fact that Shvod was thought to be Shuhat, the Syriac name of a month corresponding to February. But it is certain that originally Shvod was the name of a class of spirits.

7. For a comparative study of serpent-worship and serpent-lore see art. "Serpent" in ERE xi.

8. According to Frazer, GB, part 7, *Balder the Beautiful*, London, 1913, ix. 15, the serpent's stone is identical with the serpent's egg. This, however, is not quite certain. Nor should this egg be confused with that in which a fairy's or dragon's external soul is often hidden (*ibid.*, ii. 106f.).

9. Later magical texts use the word "dragon "in the sense of evil spirit.

10. For parallels see J. A. MacCulloch, *The Childhood of Fiction: A Study of Folk-Tales and Primitive Thought*, London, 1905, chap. 14, "The Dragon Sacrifice," and E. S. Hartland, *The Legend of Perseus*, London, 1894-96.

11. Chalatianz (p. 12) speaking of modern Armenian folk-tales about the dragons' reciprocated love for highborn matrons and maids, mentions also the fact that there are many parallels in Slav, Rumanian, and Wallachian folktales, and that it is the sons or brothers of these infatuated women who persecute the monster, often against the enamoured woman's will.

12. See art. "Changeling" in ERE iii. 358f.

13. We know ihat the Persian Azhi Dahaka, a corporeal creature and helper of Ahriman, had a human representative or could personify himself as a man.

14. Quoted by Alishan, p. 194.

15. This pulling up of the dragon out of a lake by means of oxen appears also in Celtic (Welsh) folklore.

16. In England the Lambton Worm required nine cows' milk daily. Luther, in his *Table-Talk*, describes a diabolical child--a "Killcrop"--which exhausted six nurses. The house-serpent also is often fed on milk, while in other instances the serpent is said to be disinclined to milk.

17. House-fairies (the Brownie of Scottish folk-lore) thrash as much grain in a night as twenty men can do. See Kirk, *Secret Commonwealth*, Introd. by A. Lang, p. 24.

18. There is a contradiction here. In the original Persian story the world-destroyer is the dragon himself, chained by the hero Thraetona.

19. These rocks were exposed in the morning to his eyes in order to neutralize their baleful influence during the day. The evil eye is blue. Before it, mountains, even the whole world may flame up. (Pshrank, p. 180.)

20. For whirlwinds in connection with jinn, fairies, demons, and witches see "Fairy" in ERE v. 688a.

21. Alishan, p. 66. In more recent collections of folklore, God, angels, and even the prophet Elijah, have taken the place of the ancient weather god and his helpers. The usual weapons are iron chains and the lightning. Sometimes it is a cloud-monster that is being driven hard and smitten with the lightning so that he shrieks. At other times it is the dragon hung in suspense in the sky that is trying to break his chains in order to reach and destroy the world. Angels pull him up and fasten his chains. The thunder-roll is the noise of the chains and of the affray in general. According to another and probably older account, the dragon that lives in the sea or on land, must not live beyond a

thousand years. For then he would grow out of all proportion and swallow up everything. Therefore, just before he has reached that age, angels hasten to pull him up into the sky. There he is often represented as being consumed by the sun, while his tail drops down on earth to give birth to other dragons. A magical text of more recent date speaks of the Serpent who remains in hiding for one hundred years, then is taken into the skies, like a dragon, where he acquires twelve heads and four bridles (Lkam, Arabic). The lightning is often a sword, arrow or fiery whip which the Lord is hurling at the devil, who is fleeing, and who naturally and gradually has taken the place of the ancient dragon, as the Muhammedan Shaytan crowded out the eclipse dragon.

22. Abeghian, p. 78.

23. Here, however, the meteorological dragon seems to have become fused with the eschatological dragon. Whether these two were originally identical or can be traced to different sources is an important question which need not be discussed here. See Frazer , GB8 part 7, *Balder the Beautiful*, London, 1913, i. 105 f.

24. Abbott in his *Macedonian Folk-lore* (chap. xiv.) gives a very interesting account of the dragon beliefs there, which have a close affinity both with the Indian Vrtra and the Armenian Vishap. The Macedonian dragon is a giant and a monster, terrible, voracious and somewhat stupid, but not altogether detestable. He is invariably driven away by a bride who boldly asserts herself to be " the Lightning's child, the Thunder's grandchild and a hurler of thunderbolts!" Here Indra and Vrtra are unmistakable.

25. The relation of such doctrines to the faith of the Yezidis is unmistakable (J. Menant, *Les Yezidis*, p. 83; Parry, *Six Months in a Syrian Monastery*, p. 358 f.

26. In Greek and Latin mythology the powers of Hades accept only black gifts and sacrifices, such as black sheep, heifers, beans, etc.

27. Among other things this would recall the arrows of Herakles which had been dipped in the bile of the Lemean Hydra.

28. Alishan, p. 191; Abeghian, p. 104 f.

29. Vahram Vartabed, quoted in Alishan, p. 194.

30. Perhaps the fairies' dart, which killed people and cattle in Scotland and elsewhere, is a dim reminiscence of this hunting habit of the fairies.

31. Modern Armenian folklore also knows of witches with a tail who fly to foreign lands astride upon such jars.

32. Cf. the Muslim "Brides of the Treasuries," fairy guardians of hidden treasure. Western fairies also are often imagined as mortal and as seeking to attain immortality through intermarriage with human beings. However in other instances it is they who try to free human children "from dying flesh and dull mortality" by immersing them in fairy wells. In Pshrank (p. 194), a man stumbles into a wedding of these fairies, near the ruins of a water-mill. After an oath upon the Holy Eucharist, he is allowed to taste of their wine of immortality and to take a wife from their number.

33. I owe this identification to Dr. J. W. Chapman. For the Telchins, see Blinkenberg, "Rhodische Urvolker," in Hermes, 1 [1915] pt. 2, pp. 271 ff. and the authors named by him. In an article in the *Hushartzan* (Memorial Volume) of the Mechitarists of Vienna, Nicolaos Adontz finds in Torch the Hittite god Tarqu.

34. Moses of Choren makes Torch the head of the noble house called "Angegh Tun," interpreting the word Angegh as "ugly." The expression means rather "The Vulture's House," and Torch's connection with that house is an unfounded conjecture of Moses' own or of his legendary sources.

35. See Appendix IV, The Cyclops.

36. Eznik, p. 191, Eghishe, p. 65.

37. An 11th cent. writer reports that a woman died leaving a husband and some children. While the man was perplexed as to how to take care of the orphans, a very beautiful woman appeared unexpectedly and lived with him, taking good care of him and the children. But after a while for some reason she disappeared. She was recognized as a female Dev. Modern Armenians are still catching mermaids by sticking a needle into their clothes. These can be marred or held in servitude and they will stay as long as the needle remains.

38. Eznik, p. 178.

39. Faustus, v. 2.

40. Moses, iii. 55.

41. Eznik, p. 178 f.

42. Vendidad, xviii. 45-52.

43. Under the influence of later Persian romantic conceptions of the Peris or Houris, the modern Armenian Parik has also become a most charming fairy.

44. Eznik, p. 97 f.

45. See on the modern Armenian Devs, Chalatianz, p. xiii f.; Lalayantz, "Traditions et superstitions de l' Armenie," *Revue des traditions populaires*, x. [1895] 193f; F. Macler, art. "Armenia (Christian)," in ERE i. 802; Pshrank, p. 170. Macler's is a good summary of the two preceding studies. The present-day Armenian Dev is a very large being with an immense head on his shoulders, and with eyes as large as earthen bowls. Some of them have only one eye (Pshrank, p. 170).

46. Goldziher, ARW x. [1907] 44.

47. This "mother of the Als" resembles the Teutonic devil's grandmother .

48. Quoted by Alishan, p. 222.

49. To steal unborn children is a trait of the nocturnal demon Kikimora of the Slavs also, but rather a rare notion among other peoples. The tribute mentioned in the text resembles the Scottish tradition of the similar tribute paid by the fairies to the devil, usually a human victim (see J. A. MacCulloch, artt. "Changeling," "Fairy," in ERE, iii. 360, v. 678).

50. Modern Parsis burn a fire or light in the room, probably for the same purpose. (See J. J. Modi, art. "Birth (Parsi)" in ERE ii. 661, though the writer fails to give the reason underlying this practice.)

51. The spirits of Wednesday, Friday, and Sunday eve, of which Abeghian (p. 120 f.) and, following him, Lalayantz (*Revue des traditions populaires*, x. [1895] 3), speak, are Christian inventions. Wednesday and Friday, as fast days, and Sunday as a holy day, are supposed to avenge themselves on those who do not respect their sanctity.

52. The Als are known also to modern Armenian folklore (Abeghian, p. 108 f.). But sometimes the Devs assume their functions (see Pshrank, p. 170), and they not only steal the mother's liver, but also bring the child, probably born, to their chief, substituting for him a changeling. See also Appendix V, The *Al*.

53. As this seems to be a self-contradiction, it is perhaps better to take it as a refutation by Eznik of those who said that the Nhang was a personal being.

54. In a similar manner the Teutonic Nixies showed themselves in the form of bulls and horses, and lured men maliciously into the abyss. (S. Reinach, *Orpheus*, Eng. trans., London, 1909, p. 133).

55. Alishan, p. 62 f.

56. Faustus, v. 36.

57. See p. 71.

58. Eznik, p. 98 f. It is difficult to tell whether these beneficent spirits belonged to the original stock of Armenian beliefs or whether they were a survival of the Urartian or even Babylonian spirit world. Plato does not mention them in his brief and philosophical "Er" myth, although how the dead hero's body was taken up whole (intact), without some process of healing, is hard to see. The myth about a slain hero's return to life is, however, rather foreign to Greek thought, and this trait may not have reached him at all. G. H. Basmajian, an Armenian Assyriologist, in his short *Comparative Study of our Aralez and the Babylonian Marduk* (Venice, 1898), points out that Marduk had four dogs, Ukkumu, "the snatcher," Akkulu, " the eater," Iksuda, " the snatcher," and Iltepu, "the satisfier," and that he himself is said in a cuneiform fragment from Koyunjuk, now in the British Museum (K. 8961), " to recall the dead to life," and (line 10) "to give life to the dead bodies." Yet this view, which had already been held by Emine and V.

Langlois (*Collection des historiens anciens et modernes de l' Armenie*, Paris, 1867-9, i. 26, note 1), cannot be said to be the last word on this interesting but obscure point. Marduk's dogs do not lick wounds, nor is Marduk himself specially famous for restoring dead heroes to life. Licking wounds to heal them is the most important feature of these gods or dog spirits. (For a parallel see p.204 of the African section of this volume.) Prof. Sayce saw some connexion between the Arall mountain and the Armenian Aralez, while another scholar has suggested Aralu or Hades as a possible explanation. Basmajian comes perhaps nearer to the solution. Sandalgian (*Histoire documentaire de l'Armenie*, ii. 599) quotes the letter of Sargon speaking of golden keys found in the temple of Khaldis in Mutzatzir, in the form of goddesses wearing the tiara, carrying the dented harp and the circle and treading upon dogs which made faces. But the same author (pp. 754-759) says that *arales* meant for the ancient Armenians inhabitants of Arali (Summerian Hades), but later generations, having forgotten the original sense of the word, developed the myth of the Aralezes, from the last syllable which conveyed to them the meaning of lapping.

59. Alishan, p. 177 f.

60. See also Isaiah, xxxiv. 13, Jeremiah, 1.39, in the old Armenian version.

61. Alishan, p. 185.

62. The sea-bull resembles the Celtic Water-bull, the *Tarbh Uisge* of the West Highlands, which had no ears and could assume other shapes. It dwelt in lochs and was friendly to man, occasionally emerging to mate with ordinary cows. The similar *Tarroo Ushtey* of the Isle of Man begets monsters. Both have a curious resemblance to the *Bunyip*, a mythical water monster of the Australian blacks. See J. A. MacCulloch, *The Religion of the Ancient Celts*, Edinburgh, 1911, p. 189; *Mythology of All Races*, Boston, 1916, ix. 280.

63. Besides many of the above mentioned spirits, modern Armenians know at least two others, the Hotots and the Old Hags of the Swamps. The Hotots are like devils, but they are not devils. In the winter and in the spring they live in rivers and swamps. When they appear they are all covered with mire. They do not deceive men as the devils do, but they allure them by all sorts of dances, jests, and grimaces. When the unsuspecting victim follows them for the sake of being amused,--and

who can resist the temptation?--they pull and push him into their miry abode. The Old Hags of the marshes also live in pools and swamps. They are terrible to see. They are enormous, thick, and naked, with heads as big as bath-house domes, with breasts as large as lambs hanging down. Horses, oxen, buffaloes, men, children and other living beings are drawn into their watery abode and drowned by them. (Pshrank, pp. 171-172.). See also Appendix VI, "The Finger Cutters of Albania."

Chapter XII

Cosmogony, Death, and Eschatology

NOTHING certain of the old Armenian cosmogony has survived and we may well doubt they had any, seeing that a definite cosmogony is not an integral part of Indo-European mythology. The early Christian writers, as Agathangelos and Eznik, often explain how God established the earth on "nothing," which they call the Syrian view. They maintain this against those who, according to the more general Semitic (Biblical etc.) view, teach that the earth was founded on a watery abyss. Only in modern Armenian folklore do we hear about the primeval ox or bull upon whose horns the world was set and which causes earthquakes by shaking his head whenever he feels any irritation (1). Agathangelos conceives the heavens as a solid cube hanging on nothing, and the earth "compactly formed and provided with a thick bottom, standing on nothing." For all the Armenian authors the earth stands firm and is practically the whole of the world. The star-spangled heaven upon which transparent spheres were sometimes supposed to be revolving, was of little consequence.

Whether the early Armenians had a distinct cosmogony or not we find that in the Zoroastrian stage of their religion, they held the world and all that is therein to be the work of Aramazd, who, by Agathangelos, is plainly called the creator of heaven and earth. The invisible world for them was thickly populated with occult powers, gods, angels (*Hreshtak*, from the Persian *firishtak*, "messenger"), spirits, demons and demoniac monsters of many kinds. Human life, its events and end, were predestined either by divine decrees (*Hraman*, Pers. *Farman*)

105

which were unchangeable and unerring, or through their mysterious connection with stars, constellations, and the zodiacal signs. We do not know positively, but it is very likely, that the stars were thought to be the *fravashi* (double, the external soul or self) of human beings. In modern folklore whenever a shooting star drops, a human being dies. In a word, the old Armenians were thorough-going fatalists. This view of life was so deeply rooted, and proved so pernicious in its effects, that the early Christian writers strenuously endeavored to destroy it by arguments both theological and praetical.

Man was composed of a body (*marmin*) and a soul (*hogi* or *shunch*, "breath," GXXX). *Uru*, the Iranian *urva*, may have originally been used also in the sense of soul, but it finally came to mean a phantom or a ghostly appearance. Ghosts were called *uruakan*, i.e., ghostly creatures. That these spirits received a certain kind of worship is undeniably attested by the old word *uruapast*, "ghost-worshippers," applied by Agathangelos to the heathen Armenians. The linguistic evidence shows that originally the soul was nothing more than "breath," although this conception was gradually modified into something more personal and substantial. It was never called a "shade," but in Christian times it was closely associated with light, a view which has a Zoroastrian tinge. Death was the separation or rather extraction of the soul—a more or less subtile material— from the body, through the mouth. This has always been conceived as a painful process, perhaps owing to the belief that the soul is spread through the whole body. The "soul-taking" angel and the "writer" (2) are nowadays the principal actors in this last and greatest tragedy of human life. After death the soul remains in the neighbourhood of the corpse until burial has taken place. The lifeless body usually inspires awe and fear. It is quickly washed and shrouded, and before and after this, candles and incense burn in the death-room, perhaps not so much to show the way to the disembodied and confused soul (Abeghian) as to protect the dead against evil influences. They may also be a remnant of ancestor-worship, as the saturday afternoon candles and incense are. Death in a home necessitates the renewal of the fire, as the presence of the dead body pollutes the old one. In ancient times the weeping over the dead had a particularly violent character. All the kinsmen hastened to gather around the deceased man. The dirge-mothers, a class of hired women, raised the dirge and sang his praises. The nearest relatives wept bitterly, tore their hair, cut their faces and arms, bared and beat their chests, shrieked and reproached the departed friend for the distress that he had caused by his decease. It is very probable that they cut also their long flowing hair as a sign of mourning, just as the monks, who, technically speaking, are spiritual mourners (*abegha* from the Syriac *abhila* did) at the very beginning of their taking the ecclesiastical orders. The dead were carried to their graves upon a bier. We have no mention whatever of cremation among the Armenians. On the open grave of kings and other grandees a large number of servants and women committed suicide (as happened at the death of Artaxias) to the great displeasure of his ungrateful son, Artavasd. The fortified city of Ani in Daranaghi contained the mausoleums of the Armenian kings. These were once opened by the Scythians, who either expected to find great treasures in them or intended by this barbarous method to force a battle with the retreating natives.

The hankering of the spirits for their ancient home and their "wander-lust" are well known to the Armenians. The many prayers and wishes for the "rest" of the departed soul, as well as the multitudinous funeral meals and food-offerings to the dead, show the great anxiety with which they endeavored to keep the soul in the grave. The gravestones were often made in the form of horses and lambs, which perhaps symbolized the customary sacrifices for the dead, and even now they often have holes upon them to receive food and drink offerings. Even the rice-soup in which the *pitaras* (ancestral souls) of the ancient Indians (Hindus) delighted is recalled by the present of rice which in some localities friends bring to the bereaved house on the day following the burial.

Like the Letts, Thracians, Greeks, and many other peoples, the Armenians also passed from a wild sorrow to a wilder joy in their funeral rites. This is proved by the boisterous revels of ancient times around the open grave, when men and women, facing each other, danced and clapped hands, to a music which was produced by horns, harps, and a violin (4). There was and is still a regular funeral feast in many places (5).

It is very difficult to give a clear and consistent description of the Armenian beliefs in regard to life after death. There can be no doubt that they believed in immortality. But originally, just as in Greece and other lands, no attempt was made to harmonize divergent and even contradictory views, and contact with Zoroastrianism introduced new elements of confusion. The ordinary Armenian word for grave is *gerezman*, which is nothing else but the Avestic *garo-nmana* (" house of praise," i.e., the heavenly paradise as the place of eternal light, and as the happy abode of Ahura Mazda (6). The use of this important word by the Armenians for the grave may be simply a euphemism, but it may also be expressive of an older belief in happiness enjoyed or torture suffered by the soul in the grave, very much like the foretaste of paradise or hell which is allotted to the Mohammedan dead, according to their deserts. If this be the case, the departed soul's main residence is the grave itself in the neighbourhood of the body. This body itself is greatly exposed to the attack of evil spirits.

There are also marked traces of a belief in a Hades. The Iranian Spenta Armaiti (later Spentaramet), "the genius of the earth," occurs in Armenian in the corrupt form of Santaramet and only in the sense of Hades or Hell. The Santarametakans are the dwellers in Santaramet, i.e. the evil spirits. Even the Avesta betrays its knowledge of some such older and popular usage when it speaks of the "darkness of Spenta Armaiti " (7). The earth contained Hades, and the spirit of the earth is naturally the ruler of it. Nor is this a singular phenomenon, for the earth goddesses and the vegetation gods in Western Asia and in the Graeco-Roman world have this indispensable relation to the underworld. Demeter the Black of Arcadia, or her daughter and duplicate, Persephone, forms the reverse side of Demeter, the beautiful and generous. Sabazios (Dionysos) in the Thracian world was also an underworld ruler (as Zalmoxis?). The Armenian language possesses also the word *ouydn* as the name of the ruler of Hades. This is clearly Aidonreus, or Hades. But it is difficult to ascertain whether it is an Armenized form or a cognate of these Greek names.

Another word which the Armenian Old Testament constantly uses in the sense of Hades is *Dzhokh*, from the Persian *Duzakh*, used for Hell. However, as the Christian expression *gayank*, "station," came into use for the place where, according to the ancient Fathers of the church, the souls gather and wait in a semi-conscious condition for the day of judgment, both Santaramet and Dzhokh became designations of Hell, if indeed this had not already happened in heathen times.

There is some uncertainty in regard to the location of Hades. It may be sought inside the earth at the bottom of or, perhaps, below the grave. But, on the other hand, a saying of Eznik about the wicked who have turned their faces towards the West, although directly alluding to the location of the Christian Hell and devils, may very well be understood also of the pagan Hades. For we know that Hell is a further development of Hades, and that the Babylonians, the Greeks, and the Egyptians all sought Hades, sometimes in the earth, but more usually in the West. For all of them the setting sun shone upon the world of the dead. And we have already seen how a bit of modern Armenian folklore calls the setting sun, " the portion of the dead" (8). The life led in the grave or in Hades, however sad and shadowy, was held to be very much like the present. The dead needed food, servants, etc., as the food offerings as well as the compulsory or voluntary suicides at the graves of kings clearly show.

The Armenian accounts of the end of the world are based directly upon the Persian. First of all, the people knew and told a popular Persian story about Azdahak Byrasp (Azdahak with the 10,000 horses). According to this version Azhdahak Byrasp was the ancestor of the first ruler of the Persians. He was a communist and a lover of publicity. For him nothing belonged to anyone in particular and everything must be done in public. So he began his career with a perfidious but ostentatious goodness. Later he gave himself to astrology and he was taught magic by a familiar (?) evil spirit, who kissed his shoulders, thus producing dragons on them, or changing Azdahak himself into a dragon. Now Azhdahak developed an inordinate appetite for human flesh and for spreading the lie. Finally Hruden (Thraetona, Feridun) conquered and bound him with chains of brass. While he was conducting him to Mount Damavand, Hruden fell asleep and allowed Azhdahak to drag him up the mountain. When he awoke he led Azhdahak into a cave before which he stood as a barrier preventing the monster from coming out to destroy the world (9).

But both among the Armenians and among their northern neighbours, there arose local versions of this Zoroastrian myth, in which the traditional Azhdahak yielded his place to native heroes of wickedness and the traditional mountain was changed into Massis and Alburz. In old Armenia the dreaded monster was Artavazd, the changeling son of King Artaxias. At the burial of his father, when a multitude of servants and wives and concubines committed suicide (or were slain?) on the grave, the ungrateful and unfeeling son complained and said: "Lo! Thou hast gone and taken the whole Kingdom with thee. Shall I now rule over ruins? " Angered by this re- proach, Artaxias made answer from the grave and said :

When thou goest a-hunting
Up the venerable Massis
May the Kaches seize thee
And take thee up the venerable Massis.
There mayst thou abide and never see the light.

In fact, shortly after his accession to the throne, when he went out to hunt wild boars and wild asses, he became dizzy and falling with his horse down a precipice, disappeared. The people told about him that he was chained in a cave of Massis with iron fetters which were constantly gnawed at by two dogs. When they are broken he will come out to rule over the world or to destroy it. But the noise of the blacksmith's hammer on the anvil strengthens those chains; therefore, even in Christian times, on Sundays and festival days, the blacksmiths struck their hammers on the anvil a few times, hoping thereby to prevent Artavazd from unexpectedly breaking loose upon the world.

It is also worth noting that the story about the serpents standing upon the shoulders of Azdahak and teaching him , divination was told in Greek Mythology, of the blind Melampos and possibly of Cassandra and her clairvoyant sister, while the Armenians of the fourth century of our era asserted it of the wicked King Pap, whose fame for magic had reached even the Greek world.

Any story about a catastrophic end of the world may reasonably be followed by the description of a last judgment and of a new heaven and a new earth. But unfortunately the old records completely break down on this point.. The old Armenian knows the Persian word *ristaxez*, "resurrection," as a proper name (Aristakes). Modern Armenian folk-lore has a vivid picture of the *chinvat*-bridge which it calls the hair-bridge (10). There is the word "kingdom" for the heavenly paradise which is called also *drakht* (from the Persian *dirakht*, "tree"). The picture lacked neither fire nor Devs for the torments of the evil doers, while Santaramet and Dzhokh, once meaning Hades, had also acquired the meaning of Hell. But out of these broken and uncertain hints we cannot produce a connected picture of the Armenian conception of the events which would take place when the. world came to an end. Christian eschatology, thanks to its great resemblance to the Zoroastrian, must have absorbed the native stories on this subject. However, as a branch of the Thracian race, the Armenians must have had a strong belief in immortality and brought with them a clear and elaborate account of the future world such as we find in Plato's myth of Er (11).

Footnotes

1. See E. W. Lane, *Arabian Nights*, i., notes on the first chapter, or his *Arabian Society in the Middle Ages*, ed. by S. Lane-Poole, London, 1883, p. 106 f.; also the extravagant cosmogony in the first chapter of ath-Tha'labi's *Qisas al-'anbiya*.

2. See chap. iii., part 3, on Tyr; also Abeghian, p. 16 f., and Pshrank, p. 168.

3. Herodotus (iv. 127) tells us that the Scythians challenged Darius who was invading their country and anxiously seeking an encounter vith the retreating barbarians, to violate the graves of their kings, if he wished to force them to fight.

4. The temptation is very great to read in this light the well-known report of Herodotus (v. 4) that the Thracians mourned at a birth but vere very joyful at a death. The father of historians and folklorists, whose bias to see in everything Thracian some sign of belief in immortality was strong, may be describing a Thracian funeral only imperfectly, i.e., through the very noisy funeral-feast. The funeral-feast is and was a widely spread custom. See artt. "Death and Disposal of the Dead," ERE, iv. 411 if., "Feasting," *ibid.*, v. 801 if.; and W. Caland, *Die vorchristlichen haltischen Totengebrauche*, ARW iii.

5. For more details on burial customs among the Armenians, see Abeghian, p. 16f; Pshrank, p. 256, and "Funeral Rites" in EBr, xi. 329.

6. A. V. W. Jackson, *Die lranische Religion*, in Geiger and Kuhn, *Grundriss*, ii. 685.

7. *Vendidad*, iii. 35. Darkness was also the distinguishing feature f the house of Lie.

8. Pshrank, p. 198.

9. For the more Avestic form of this myth, see A. V. W. Jackson, *Die Iranische Religion*, in Geiger and Kuhn, *Grundriss*, ii. 663f. see also *Mythology of All Races*, Boston, 1917, vi. 320. That a dread, alarming dragon, who flies above the entire realm of air, and terrifies Jove and the other gods, as well as the powers of Hades, will bring the world to an end, is known also to'Apuleius. (Bk. iv. 33, 35.)

10. Pshrank, p. 234; Abeghian, p. 20.

11. J. A. Stewart, *The Myths of Plato*, London, 1905 (the myths of Er, *Repub.*, 613E to 621D, with parallel trans., pp. 134-151; observations on the myth of Er, pp. 152-172).

Appendices

I. Vahagn
(See Chap. V)

The conclusion that Vahagn was Agni, i.e., a fire-god in its different aspects, is difficult to escape. But what does his name mean? Windischmann, followed by Lagarde and Hubschmann, identified him with the Iranian Verethraghna, a genius of victory, on the basis of the slight resemblance between the two names and of the fact that Vahagn grants courage to his worshippers. Moreover, both Vahagn and Verethraghna were identified by ancient Hellenizers with Herakles.

Windischmann's view is untenable, not only because Verethraghna is represented in Armenia by other more unmistakable names, but also because the Vahagn myths have nothing in common with the Avestic Verethraghna, although as we have seen, both gods were identical in pre-Vedic and pre-Avestic times. Windischmann's view on this matter has so completely dominated Western scholars that no one has bestowed any thought on the Vahagn myths which we have just examined. It is true that the Avestic Verethraghna was also born in an ocean. But he does not fight against dragons nor is he closely associated with fire. (The dragon fighters of Iran are Atar, the fire, Tishtrya, the rain-star which conquers Apaosha, the Iranian genius of drought, Thraetona, and Keresaspa.) Although, as has been noticed by Avestic scholars like Lehmann, Jackson, and Carnoy, the only tangible traits of Verethraghna remind us of Indra, the individuality of his figure and of his activities is not so sharply defined as those of Vahagn or of Indra.

Moreover, it is very difficult to derive the name of Vahagn from Verethraghna. How did the strong "r's" of "Verethra" become entirely lost in a language that revels in r's, while the very weak *aghn* survived? Granting even that this is what happened, what is the place of Vahagn among such forms of Verethraghna's name as Vrtan (perhaps also Vardan) , Vahram, and Vram, which occur in Armenia?

For these reasons, as well as his manifest connection with the fire, it seems best to consider Vahagn's name as a compound of *Vah* and *Agni*. By some Sanscrit scholars this has been interpreted as Fire-bringer. The sacrificial Agni is called in the Vedas *havya-vah* or *havya-vahana* (Macdonell, p. 97). But *Vah* must have meant something else than "a bringer" to the old Armenians. It is interesting to note that all the names and adjectives derived from Vahagn use only the first syllable as if it were a divine name by itself. His temple was called the Vahevahyan temple. His priests were known as Vahunis or Vahnunis. Men claiming descent from Vahagn were often called Vahe, Vahan, and Van—a corruption of Vahan. Wackernagel (quoted by Gelzer) suggests that at his rites or mysteries, the enthused worshipper must have shouted "Vahe'vah," as at weddings Greeks shouted *umeneios* for *umen*. The resemblance would perhaps have been more striking if he had cited the case of *saboi* for *sabaxios* in the Dionysia.

If there is anything in the classical testimonies bearing upon the kinship of the Armenians with the Thracian races, and in particular with the Phrygians, one might set the ancient Phrygian satyr or rather god Hyagnis beside Vahagn. (See on Hyagnis, *La Grande Encyclopidie* and *Pauly-Wissowa, s.v.*) At first glance the similarity between the two names is just as striking as that between the Vedic and Avestic Indra, or the Vedic Nasatya and the Avestic Naonhaithya. What is more, just as "Vahagn," "Hyagnis" (the supposed father and perhaps the duplicate of Marsyas) also is a compound word, for both Agnis and *hyes* occur alone. Agnis stands for Hyagnis in the Mosaic of Monnus (*Pauly-Wissowa, loc. cit.*) and *hyes* or *hyas* is confessedly a Phrygian god. Both Aristophanes and the Assyrians knew him as such. It would seem that at the stage of development in which we meet with Hyagnis and Marsyas in Phrygian mythology, they had become divested of their original character in favor of the all-victorious Sabazios or Dionysos, becoming mere flute-players and musical inventors who adorned his procession. But the original relation of Hyagnis to the fire can be legitimately inferred from his transparent name, and Marsyas' interest in the fertilizing rivers is a commonplace of classical mythology and geography. It is not unlikely that some representation of Hyagnis with reeds as his symbol gave rise to the misapprehension that he was an inventor of the flute and other allied musical instruments. For the Greek the flute was Phrygian and every reed suggested a flute. The *Vah* of Vahagn and the *hyas* of Hyagnis are identical with *hyes* used as a name or title of Dionysos. When we consider the fact that the Greek *v* was bilabial, then we can easily see how a *v* could change into a *hy*. But we may observe the same phenomenon between other cognate languages; for example, the Greek *espera* appears as *vespera* in Latin. One may even say that between the different members of the Thracian family *h* and *v* interchanged freely. So the Phrygian word for bread given by Herodotus as *bekos* is *hatz* in Armenian. The Greeks usually, and not without some foundation, associated this word *hyes* , "Hyas," with their *hyein*", "to rain." In fact *Vah* and *Hyas* must be brought together with Vayu, the air and weather god of the Vedas (and of the Avesta) and the other self of Indra. According to Darmesteter, the Avestic Vayu fights on the side of Mithra against the Devas by means of the tempest. We may even compare the Zoroastrian *Vae i vah* ("the good Vayu") with the Armenian Vahevah mentioned above, and conclude that the resemblance is not fortuitous. On the other hand the Armenian word *aud*, "air," "weather," adequately represents the Vedic and Avestic *Vata*, which, according to Macdonell, is Vayu in its physical aspect.

The inevitable inference is that Vahagn-Hyagnis was originally a lightning god with special reference to weather and to rain, very much like the water-born Agni or the Apam Napat as well as the Lithuanian Sventa Ugnele (Holy Fire) who bears the title of *Visiya*, "the fruit bringer" or "increase giver" (ARW i. 368), which is a clear reference to his relation to the rain.

A. von Gutschmid finds that the Armenian legend about St. Athenogene, who took the place of Vahagn in Ashtishat, has a peculiar relation to game and hunting. From this he has

115

inferred that among other things Vahagn was the patron of game and hunting. This theory finds a partial confirmation in Adiabene, southeast of Armenia, where Herakles was adored and invoked as the god of the hunters. (Gutschmid, iii. 414.) This Herakles may be Vahagn, but more probably it is Verethraghna, whose worship also has spread westward.

Moses tells us that Vahagn was worshipped in Iberia also and sacrifices were offered before his large statue. (i. 31.) A euhemerized but very interesting form of the Agni myth is found in the Heimskringla, or chronicles of the kings of Norway, by Snorro Sturleson (see English translation by Sam. Laing, London, 1844, i. 33 f.). Agne (fire) is the son of King Dag (day), who was slain in his ship in the evening. Agne overcomes the Finnish chief Froste (cold) in a battle and captures his son Loge (Luke, Lewk?) and his daughter Skialf (" shivering "). The latter, whom Agne had married, contrived to avenge the death of her father in the following manner: Agne, on her own instance, gave a burial feast in honor of her father, and having drunk copiously, fell asleep. Thereupon she attached a noose to the golden ornament about his neck, the tent was pulled down, and Agne was dragged out, hauled up, and hanged close to the branches of a tree. He was buried in Agnefit.

According to this naturalistic myth, fire is related to the day and therefore to the sun. It conquers the cold and is conquered in turn by it, and being extinguished, it returns to the tree (its mother?). This is another echo of the ancient fire-myths.

II. Witchcraft and Magic

(See Chap. VI)

The ancient Armenians were much given to witchcraft and divination. John Mantaguni (5th century) mentions no less than twenty-five forms of magical practices. Eznik's short notices on bringing down the moon remind us of the same practice among the Thessalians, so often spoken of by Latin writers, such as Apuleius, Horace, Petronius, etc. Horace says:

Non defuisse masculae libidinis
Ariminensem Foliam
Et otiosa credidit Neapolis
Et omne vicinum oppidum
Quae sidera excantata voce Thessala
Lunamque coelo deripit.

[If idle Naples and each neighboring city Rightly believe, the Ariminian hag, Unnatural Folia, failed not that grim conclave, She who could draw the moon and subject stars, With her Thessalian witch-song, down from heaven.]

This was a most difficult feat performed by the witch, either as an expression of anger or as an exhibition of great skill.

Bringing down the moon is found in Chinese encyclopedias as a favorite trick of Taoist doctors. The following quotations were furnished by Prof. Hodous of the Kennedy School of Missions, Hartford, Conn.: According to the *Hsuan Shih Chi*, written during the T'ang dynasty, "In the T'ang dynasty in the reign of T'ai Ho (827-836 A.D.) a certain scholar named Chow possessed a Taoist trick. At the mid-autumn festival he met with his guests. At the time the moon was very bright. He said to his guests when they were seated, 'I am able to cut off the moon and place it into my sleeve.' In order to do this he commanded them to empty the room. He took several hundred chopsticks, tied them with a string, and mounted them saying, 'I am about to climb up and take the moon.' Suddenly they noticed that heaven and earth were darkened. Then he opened the room and said, 'The moon is in the dress of Mr. N. N.' Then with his hand he raised the dress. Out of a fold of the dress there came out a moon over an inch in diameter. Suddenly the whole house was very bright and the cold penetrated the muscles and bones."

The *Yu Yang Tsa Tsu*, written towards the end of the eighth century, records another instance: "In the beginning of the reign of Ch'ang K'ing (821-825 A.D.) a hermit called Yang was in Tch'eu Chow (Hunan). It was his custom to seek out those who were searching after the Tao. There was a local scholar called T'ang. The natives called him a man a hundred years old. Yang went to him and he persuaded him to stop a night. When night came he called a girl saying: 'Bring the last quarter of the moon.' The girl pasted a piece of paper like the moon on the wall. T'ang arose and bowed to it saying: 'Tonight there is a guest here, you should give him light.' When he finished speaking the whole house was as bright as if he had hung up candles."

It is suggested that the magicians performed this wonder by means of mirrors.

Armenian magical texts of a later date tell us that the sorcerers climbed up a ladder of hair to tie the moon to the mountain top and the sun to its mother!

III. Additional Note on Semiramis

(See Chap. X)

In the Noldeke Festschrift, Lehmann-Haupt has shown that the Assyrian queen Sammuramat (fl.c. 800 B.C.), probably a Babylonian by birth, is the historical figure about whom the legendary story of Semiramis has gathered. But this does not account for the fact that the Semiramis of legend has characteristics which unmistakably belong to the goddess Istar, and that in the story, as Ctesias tells it, she is connected with north Syria, the seat, in Graeco-Roman times, of the worship of the Syrian (= Assyrian) goddess. Yet a third factor in the legend (cf. A. Ungnad, OLZ (1911], 388), seems to be a reminiscence of the very ancient Babylonian queen Azag-Bau, who is said to have founded the dynasty of Kish.

The Semiramis of Herodotus (i. 184) is clearly the historical Sammuramat; in Ctesias, the supernatural birth of the great queen and her disappearance from the earth in the form of a dove (Assyr. *shummu*) is just as unmistakably mythological; yet a third version of the story, that of Deinon (Aelian, vii. I, i), according to which Semiramis is a *hetaera*, who having won the affections of King Ninus, asks leave to rule for five days, and when once she is in possession of the government puts the king

118

to death, is pure folklore. Yet Deinon's account reminds us of Azag-Bau, for Babylonian tradition made the latter "a female liquor-seller "—in so far corresponding to the Greek *hetaera,* and in the omen-tablets we read: "When a child is bisexual, that is an omen of Azag-Bau, who ruled over the land." This idea underlies the version adopted by Ctesias: "Ein Mannweib, die Semiramis, hatte das Reich gegrundet; ein weibischer Mann (the legendary Sardanapalus) brachte es ins Verderben" (Duncker, *Gesch. des Attertums,* iii. p. 353).

The mutual relationship of the three chief variants of the story would be explained, if we suppose that Sammuramat was originally an epithet of the goddess Istar, or possibly of the primeval queen Azag-Bau; compare the Gilgamesh Epic, vi. 13, where Istar says to the hero: "Thou shalt enter into our dwelling amid the sweet odors (sammati) of cedar-wood." Semiramis would then mean "fond of sweet odors." There is, however, another etymology, which is also of ancient date, *summu ramat,* "fond of the dove," the dove being the sacred bird of Ishtar (Diodorus, ii. 4). See Alfred Jeremias, *Izdubar-Nimrod,* pp. 68-70. W. J. CHAPMAN

The Armenians ascribed the Urartian works in Van, especially a mighty dam, to Semiramis' building activities. She is supposed to have chosen that city as her summer residence. The saga reported that she died in Armenia. As she was pursued by her armed enemies, she fled afoot, but being exceedingly thirsty she stooped to drink water (from a source) when she was overtaken by her enemies. How she died is not clear, but the sagas spoke of the enchanting of the sea, and of the beads (?) of Shamiram in the sea. There was also a stone called Shamiram, which, according to Moses, was prior to the rock of the weeping Niobe. Those who are acquainted with the classical form of the Semiramis legend will easily perceive how the Armenians have appropriated the details about her building palaces and water-canals in Media and her death in India.

See also on Semiramis, Lenormant,

La Legende de Semiramis, Brussels [1873]; Sayce, "The Legend of Semiramis," *Hist. Rev.,* 1888; Art. "Semiramis" in EBr 9th and 11th ed; Frazer, GB, iii, 161 ff.; Uhlrich Wilcken, *Hermes*, xxviii [1893], 161 ff., 187 ff.; F. Hommel, *Gesch. Bab. u. Assyr.*, Berlin [1885], pp. 630-632; C. F. Lehmann-Haupt in Noldeke *Festschrift*. For the Assyrian text see Walter Andrae, *Die Stehlenreihen in Assur*, Leipzig [1913], p. 11, and compare Lehmann-Haupt, *Die historische Semiramis und ihre Zeit*, Tubingen [1910].

IV. The Cyclops

(See Chap. XI)

The Cyclops, and especially Polyphemos, are to be found everywhere in Europe and Asia (see e.g. W. C. Grimm, "Die Sage von Polyphem," ABAW, 1857, p. 1 ff.; J. and W. Grimm, *Kinder und Hausmiirchen*, NO. 130; W. R. S. Ralston, *Russian Folk Tales*, London, 1873, ch. iii; Herodotus, on the Arimaspians, iv. 27; G. Krek, *Einleitung in die Slavische Litteraturgeschichte*; Graz, 1887, pp. 665-759; G. Polivka, "Nachtrage zur Polyphemsage," ARW i. [1898] 305 f.). The black giant whom Sinbad the Sailor, Odysseus-like, blinded on his third voyage, is well known to readers of the *Arabian Nights*. Polyphemos appears also in Russian folklore, with the name of Licko, with the sheep under which his tormentor escapes, and with his cry, "No man has done it," while he is bewailing his lost eye. It is perfectly evident that certain important details, such as the one single round eye and the burning of it, have disappeared from the rationalizing and short Armenian account. The modern descendants of the Cyclops in Armenia are one-eyed beings, who are either gigantic devils or a monstrous race living in caves. Each individual weighs a hundred times more than a human being. In the day-time they sit on their roofs in wait for travellers, animals, birds, jinn, monsters, whom they may devour. When nothing comes they procure a whole village for their dinner. For other versions of the Cyclops story, see J. A. MacCulloch, *The Childhood of Fiction*, London, 1905, Chap. 10.

V. The Al

(See Chap. XI)

A magical text of uncertain date says: "St. Peter, St. Paul and Silas while they were travelling, saw on the roadside a man sitting on the sand. His hair was like snakes, his eyebrows were of brass, his eyes were of glass, his face was as white as snow, his teeth were of iron, and he had a tusk like a wild boar. They asked him: 'What art thou, impure, accursed and awful beast, etc. ? ...' He answered : 'I am the wicked Al. I sit upon the child-bearing mother, I scorch her ears and pullout her liver (?) and I strangle both mother and child. Our food is the flesh of little children and the liver (?) of mothers with child. We steal the unborn infants of eight months from the mother and we carry them, deaf and dumb, to our King. The abyss, the corners of the houses and of stables are our habitation.'"

Another magical text says: St. Sisi (Sisoe) and St Sisiane (Sisinnios), St. Noviel and the angel St. Padsiel had gone a-hunting with the permission of Christ. They heard the cry of an infant and going in its direction, they surprised the Al in its evil work. They caught him and bound him to the Al-stone. Thereupon came the mother of the Al and they said: "What does it mean that you enter the womb of mothers, eat the flesh and drink the blood of infants and change the light of their eyes into darkness, etc."

Mher

Mher was the son of the Hero David. While avenging his father, he sees before him an open door which he enters with his fiery horse and the door closes behind him. Ever since that day Mher lives in that cave. The underground river Gail (Lukos) flows under the cave with a terrible rumbling. Once a year (either on the festival of Roses, originally a fire and water festival, or in the night of the ascension identified with the night of destinies) Mher's door is opened. Anyone near-by enters and is led by Mher to his great treasures, where the poor man forgetting himself allows the door to be closed upon him. Some day Mher

121

will come out of the cave, mounted on his fiery horse, to punish the enemies of his people. That will be the *dies irae* for which the Armenians of the Van region wait with impatience.

VI. The Finger-Cutters of [Caucasian] Albania [Atrpatakan/Aghuania]

Moses of Kalankata, in his history of Albania (in Armenian, pp. 39-42), describes a sect of "finger-cutters " which has unmistakable affinities with devil-worship and witchcraft. Vatchakan, the King of Albania in the last quarter of the 5th Century, was a zealous persecutor of all heresies and of heathen practices. He was especially endeavoring to uproot the "finger-cutters," when a boy came to him with the report that while he was crossing the pine-woods on the bank of the River Cyr, he saw that a multitude of people had stretched a boy on the ground, and having bound him to four pegs by his thumbs and large toes, they flayed him alive. As they descried the stranger, they pursued him in order to use him also as a victim; but he fled from them, and leaping into the river swam to an islet where he climbed a tree, and, unseen by his pursuers, he observed the whole procedure, but more particularly those who participated in this bloody rite. These he denounced to the King by name. They were arrested by his command and put to torture, but no confession could be extorted from them. As they were all being led to the place of execution, the King singled out a young man among them, and through the promise of life and freedom, finally induced him to confess what took place at the secret gatherings.

The following is the testimony given by this young man: "The devil comes in the form of a man and commands the people to stand in three groups. One of these (?) must hold the victim without wounding or slaying him. The whole skin is taken off along with the thumb of the right hand and carried over across the chest to the little finger of the left hand, which is also cut off and taken along. The same process is repeated on the feet, while the victim is alive. Thereupon he is put to death; the skin is freed from the body, prepared and laid in a basket. When the time of the evil worship arrives, they make (set up?) a folding chair of iron (sic!) with feet which closely resemble the feet of that man (or the feet of man?). They place a precious garment on the chair. The devil comes, puts on this garment and sits on the chair and having taken the skin of the human sacrifice along with the fingers, he is seen (becomes visible?). If they are unable to bring him the customary tribute [of a human skin], he commands them to peel off the bark of a tree. They also sacrifice before him cattle and sheep, of whose flesh he partakes in the company of his wicked ministers. [Further] they saddle a horse which they keep ready for him. This he rides and gallops off until the horse comes to a stop. There the devil vanishes. This he does once a year."

The King commanded the young man to repeat this ghastly ceremony on the prisoners themselves before the royal army. Many of them were thus flayed and murdered in the presence of their own families. There were slain on that day many poisoners. For it was a practice of the members of that Sect that each (?) one should, on the devil's command, poison some one [during the year?]. If he was unable to find a victim, the devil harassed him so persistently that he finally gave the poison to a member of his own family. Those that were slothful in these religious duties or denounced anyone [of the devil worshippers to the authorities] were visited by the devil with blindness and leprosy.

Bibliography

I. Abbreviations

ABAW
Abhandlungen Koniglich-Preussische Akademie der Wissenschaften zu Berlin.

ARW
Archiv fur Religionswissenschaft.

EBr11
Encyclopedia Britannica, 11th ed.

ERE
Encyclopedia of Religion and Ethics.

OLZ
Orientalische Litteraturzeitung.

SBE
Sacred Books of the East.

SWAW Sitzungsberichte der Wiener Akademie der Wissenschaften.

TICO
Transactions of the International Congress of Orientalists, London, 1893.

VKR
Verhandlungen des zweiten internat. Kongresses fur allgemein. Religionsgeschichte, Basel, 1905.

II. Encyclopedias

Daremberg, V., and Saglio, E., *Dictionnoire des antiquites grecques et romaines*, Paris, 1887 ff.

ENCYCLOPEDIA BRITTANICA, Cambridge, 11th ed., 1910-11.

ENCYCLOPEDIA OF RELIGION AND ETHICS, ed. J. Hastings, Edinburgh, 1908ff.

Ersch, J. S. and J. G. Gruber, *Allgemeine Encyklopadie der Wissenschaften und Kunste*, Leipzig, 1818-50.

GRANDE ENCYCLOPEDIE, LA, Paris, 1885-1901.

PAULY, A. F. von, *Realencyclopadie der classischen Altertumrwissenschaft*, New ed. by G. Wissowa, Stuttgart, 1904ff.

ROSCHER, W. H., *Ausfuhrliches Lexicon der griechische und romische Mythologie*, Leipzig, 1884-1902.

III. Sources

For the Indo-European period down to Christian times the most important native sources are:

AGATHANGELOS, 5th cent., ed. Venice, 1865.

ANANIA OF SHIRAG, 7th cent., ed. Patkanean, Petrograd, 1877.

EZNIK, 5th cent., ed. Venice, 1826.

EGHISHE (ELISAEUS), 5th cent., ed. Venice.

FAUSTUS OF BYZANTIUM, 5th cent., ed. Venice, 1869, also in V. Langlois, *Collection des historiens anciens et modernes de l'Armenie*, Paris, 1857-9.

MOSES OF CHOREN, 5th cent., *History and Geography of Armenia*, ed. Venice, 1865.

OHAN MANTAGUNI, 5th cent., ed. Venice.

The ancient Armenian version of the Old Testament is useful for names. We also gather short but valuable notices from Xenophon's *Anabasis*, Strabo's *Geography*, and the works of Dio Cassius, Pliny, and Tacitus. Alishan has gathered in his *Ancient Faith of Armenia* (in Armen.), Venice, 1895, a good deal of very valuable material from edited and unedited works of the medieval writers. The Armenian language itself is one of the richest sources of information, along with the church ritual and scientifically collected folklore. Among the latter we may name Abeghian, *Armenischer Volksglaube*, Pshrank, *Crumbs from the Granaries of Shirak*, and parts of Srvantzdian's *Manana* (see under IV. Literature).

IV. Literature

Besides many articles in ARW, EBr, ERE, Daremberg et Saglio, Pauly-Wissowa, Roscher, and *La Grande Encyclopedie*, the following works may be noted.

ABEGHIAN, M., *Armenischer Volksglaube*, Leipzig, 1899.

AHARONIAN, A., *Les croyances des anciens Armeniens*, Geneva, 1912.

ALISHAN, L., *Ancient Faith of the Armenians* (Armen.), Venice,1895.

ARAKELIAN, H., *La religion ancienne des Armeniens* in VKR, p. 291f.

ASLAN, K., *Etudes historiques sur le peuple armenien*, Paris, 1909.

BALASSANIAN, S., *History of Armenia* (Armen.), Tiflis, 1896.

BASMAJIAN, G., *Critical Study of our Aralez and the Babylonian Marduk*, Venice, 1898.
-*True History of Armenia*, Constantinople, 1914.

CARRIERE, A., *Les huit sanctuaires de l'Armenie payenne*, Paris, 1899. This influential study is available on another page of this website in English translation, The Eight Sanctuaries of Pagan Armenia.

CASSEL, P., *Drachenkampfe*, Berlin, 1868.

CHALATIANZ, G., *Marchen und Sagen*, Leipzig, 1887.

CHANTEPIE DE LA SAUSSAYE, P. D., *Lehrbuch der Religions-geschichte*, Tubingen, 1905.

CUMONT, F., *Die Mysterien des Mithra*, Leipzig, 1903.
-*Texts et monuments figures relatifs aux mysteres de Mithra*, Brussels, 1896-9.

DAGHAVARIAN, N., *Ancient Religions of the Armenians* (Armen.), in *Banasser*, 1903.

DAVIS, GLADYS M. N., *The Asiatic Dionysos*, London, 1914.

DER-MESROBIAN, S., *Critical History of Armenia*, Venice, 1914.

DOLENS, N., and KHATCH, A., *Histoire des anciens Armeniens*, Geneva, 1907.

EMIN, M., *Recherche sur le paganisme armenien*, in *Revue de l'Orient*, N.S. v. 18.
-*Moses of Khoren and the Old Epicss of the Armenians*, Tifiis, 1886.

ERMAN, A., *Handbook of Egyptian Religion*, tr. A. S. Griffith, London, 1907.

FARNELL, L. R., *The Cults of the Greek States*, Oxford, 1896-1909.

FRAZER, J. G., *The Golden Bough*, London, 1907-15.

GEIGER, W., and KUHN, E., *Grundriss der iranische Philologie*, Strassburg, 1895-1904.

GELZER, H., *Zur armenische Gotterlehre, in Berichte der Koniglich-Siichsischen Gesellschaft der Wissenchaften, phil. hist. Classe.*, 1895, pp. 99-148.

GUTSCHMID, A. VON, *Kleine Schriften*, Leipzig, 1889-94.

HOMMELL, F., *Grundriss der Geographie und Geschichte des alten Orients*, Munich, 1904.

HUBSCHMANN, H., *Armenische Grammatik*, Leipzig, 1897.

Hushartzan (A collection of essays by various scholars), Vienna, 1911.

INJIJIAN, L., *Armenian Archaeology*, Venice, 1835.

JACKSON, A. V. W., *Iranische Religion*, in Geiger-Kuhn, *Grundriss d. iran. Philologie*, Vol. ii.

JASTROW, M., *Die Religion Babyloniens und Assyriens*, Giessen, 1905-12.

JENSEN, P., *Hittiter und Armenier*, Strassburg, 1898.

KARAKASHIAN, A., *Critical History of Armenia* (Armen.) Tifiis, 1895.

LAGARDE, P., *Armenische Studien*, Gottingen, 1887.
-*Purim*, Gottingen, 1887.

LANGLOIS, V., *Collections des historiens anciens et modernes de l'Armenie*, Paris, 1867-69.

MACDONELL, A. A., *Vedic Mythology*, Stuttgart, 1897.

MAEHLY, J., *Die Schlange in Mythus und Kultus*, Basel, 1867.

MEYER, E., *Geschichte des Alterthums*, Berlin, 1909.

MOORE, G. F., *History of Religions*, vol. i, Edinburgh, 1914.
MOULTON, J. H., *Early Zoroastrianism*, London, 1913.

NAZARETIAN, *Armenians and Armenian Mythology* (Armen.), in *BAZMAWEP*, 1893-4.

OLDENBERG, H., *Die Religion des Veda*, Berlin, 1894.

PATON, L. B., *Spiritism and the Cult of the Dead in Antiqutty*, New York, 1921.

PATRUBANI, *Beitriige zur Armenischen Etymologie*, Budapest, 1897.

PSHRANK, *Crumbs from the Granaries of Shirak*, a collection of eastern Armenian folklore.

SAHAG-MESROB, *Urartu*, Constantinople, 1909.

SANDALGIAN, J., *Histoire documentaire de l'Armenie*, Paris, 1917.

SARKISSIAN, B., *Agathangelos and his Many-centuried Mystery* (Armen.), Venice, 1892.

SCHRADER, 0., *Arische Religion*, Leipzig, 1914.

SEROPIAN, BsHP. M., *Armenia and Hayastan*, n. d.

SIECKE, E., *Drachenkiimpfe*, Leipzig, 1907.

SRVANTZDIAN, *Manana*.

STOCKELBERG, "Iranian Influence on the Religious Beliefs of

the Ancient Armenians," in *Report of the Imperial Archaeological Society of Moscow, Oriental Comm.* (Russian), ii. pt. 2, Moscow, 1901.

TCHIRAZ, M., *Notes sur la mythologie armenienne*, in TICO, ii., London,1893.

TISDALL, W. ST. CLAIR, *The Conversion of Armenia to the Christian Faith*, Oxford, 1897.

UNGUAD, A., *Das Gilgemesch-Epos*, Gottingen, 1911.

WEBER, S., *Die Katholische Kirche in Armenien*, Freiberg, 1903.

WINDISCHMANN, F., *Die persische Anahita oder Anaitis*, in *Abhandlungen der Konig. Bayr. Akadamie der Wissenchaften*, i. *Classe*, viii. pt. 1, Munich, 1856.

V.

A large number of works on Folklore have been used, among which the following may be named.

ABBOTT, G. F., *Maccdonian Folk-Lore*, Cambridge, 1907.

CONWAY, M. D., *Demonology and Devil Lore*, New York, 1879.

CROOKE, W., *The Popular Religion and Folklore of Northern India*, London,1897.

HARTLAND, E. SYDNEY, *The Legend of Perseus*, London, 1896.

KIRK, REv. R., *The Secret Commonwealth of Elves, Fauns, and Fairies*, ed. A Lang, London, 1893. LANE, E. W., *An Account of the Manners and Customs of the Modern Egyptians. -Arabian Society in the Middle Ages*, ed. S. Lane Poole, London, 1883.

RALSTON, W. R. S., *Russian Folk-tales*, London, 1873.

RHYS, SIR JOHN, *Celtic Folk-lore*, Oxford, 1891.

WENTZ, W. Y. E., *The Fairy Faith in Celtic Countries*, Oxford, 1911.

WUNDT, W. M., *Elemente der Volkerpsychologie*, Leipzig, 1913.

Also the following articles:

"Dragon", in *Daremberg-Saglio*.
"Phrygians," in ERE ix.
"Serpent," in *New Schaff-Herzog Encyclopedia of Religious Knowledge*.
"Serpent Worship," in EBr.

VI. Principal Articles Connected with Armenian Mythology in the *Encyclopedia of Religion and Ethics* (Vols. I-XII)

ANAN1KIAN, M., "Armenia (Zoroastrian)," i. 794-802.

CARNOY, A. J., "Magic (Iranian)," viii. 293-6.

CASARTELLI, L. C., "Charms and Amulets (Iranian)," iii. 448. -"Dualism (Iranian)," V. I 11-2.

CRAWLEY, A. E., "Fire and Fire-Gods," vi. 26-30.

CUMONT, F., "Anahita," i. 414-5. —"Art (Mithraic)," i. 872-4. —"Architecture (Mithraic)," i. 744-5.

EDWARDS, E., "Altar (Persian)," i. 346-8. —"God (Iranian)," vi. 290-4.
—"Priest, Priesthood (Iranian)," x. 319-22.

GRAY, L. H., "Achaemenians," i. 69-73.
—"Barsom," ii. 424-5.
—"Blest, Abode of the (Persian)," ii. 702-4.

131

SAYCE, A. H., "Armenia (Vannic)," i. 793-4.
—"Median Religion," viii. 514-5.

SODERBLOM, N., "Ages of the World (Zoroastrian)," i. 205-10.

The Eight Sanctuaries
of Pagan Armenia

By Auguste Carri

According to Agat'angeghos and Movses Xorenats'i
[Les huit sanctuaires de l'Arménie payenne]
Paris, 1899, English Translation by Robert Bedrosian, 2009

I

If Movses Xorenats'i is to be believed, Artashes I was the grandson and second successor of Vagharshak, founder of the Armenian Arsacid dynasty. He was a warrior king who conquered Asia Minor, invaded Greece, and "filled the Ocean with the multitude of his ships." He died in a military coup, during which his innumerable soldiers killed each other (MX II. 11-13). Artashes left the throne to his son Tigran, who was the son-in-law and ally of Mithridates, and the adversary of Lucullus and Pompey, who extended his conquests to Mesopotamia and Syria.

During his campaigns Artashes had found in Asia Minor and Greece a certain number of statues of the gods which he took back to Armenia to install in the native sanctuaries as victory trophies. Tigran, who had realized his father's aspirations, also enriched these sanctuaries with the addition of a statue found in Mesopotamia.

Here are the passages from Movses Xorenats'i describing these events:

1.

Finding in Asia images of Artemis, Heracles, and Apollo that were cast in bronze and gilded, he had them brought to our country to be set up in Armavir. The chief priests, who were of the Vahuni family, took those of Apollo and Artemis and set them up in Armavir; but the statue of Heracles, which had been made by Scyllas and Dipenes of Crete, they supposed to be Vahagn their ancestor and so set it up in Tarawn in their own village of Ashtishat after the death of Artashes. MX II. 12, p. 148.

Եւ գտեալ յԱսիայ պղնձաձոյլ ոսկեզոծ պատկերս զԱրտեմիդեայ եւ զՀերակլեայ եւ զԱպողոնի՝ տայ բերել յաշխարհս մեր, զի կանգնեցեն յԱրմաւիր։ Զոր առեալ քրմապետացն, որ էին յազգէն Վահունեաց՝ զԱպողոնին եւ զԱրտեմիդեայն կանգնեցին յԱրմաւիր. իսկ զՀերակլեայն գառնապատկերն, որ արարեալ էր ի Սկիւդեայ եւ ի Դիփինոսէ կրետացւոյ, զՎահագն իւրեանց վարկանելով նախնի՝ կանգնեցին ի Տարոն, յիւրեանց սեպհական գիւղն յԱշտիշատ, յետ մահուանն Արտաշիսի։

2.

He also took from Hellas images of Zeus, Artemis, Athena, Hephaistos, and Aphrodite, and had them brought to Armenia. But before they had arrived in our land the sad news of Artashes' death was heard. [Those bringing them] fled and brought the images to the fortress of Ani *. The priests followed and stayed with them. MX II. 14, p. 149.

Բայց եւ յԵլլադայ առեալ պատկերս զԴիոսի, զԱրտեմիդեայ, զԱթենայ, զՀեփեստու, զԱփրոդիտեայ՝ տայ բերել ի Հայս. որք ոչ ժամանեալ միջամուխ լինել յաշխարհս՝ լսեն զբօթ մահուանն Արտաշիսի. եւ փախուցեալ ընկենուն զպատկերսն յամրոցն յԱնի. եւ քուրմք զնոցին զհետ լինելով, դադարեն առ նոսա։

---

* One must not confuse the fortress of Ani (also called Kamakh; on modern maps, Kemakh) situated on the left bank of the Euphrates in Upper Armenia, with the city of Ani on the Axurian River, in the province of Ararat which was the capital of the Bagratid kingdom and whose ruins are well known. Cf. Saint-Martin, *Mémoires sur l'Arménie*, I, p. 72 and 111 ff.

3.

As his first task he wished to construct the temples. But the priests, who had come from Greece, decided not to penetrate deep into Armenia. For an excuse they feigned omens to the effect that the gods wished to reside at that very spot. Tigran consented and raised the statue of Zeus Olympus in the fortress of Ani, that of Athena in T'il, the second statue of Artemis in Ere'z [†], and that of Hephaistos in Bagayr'inj. But the statue of Aphrodite, as the beloved of Heracles, he ordered to be set up beside the statue of the same Heracles in Ashtishat. And angered at the Vahuni in that they had taken it upon themselves to set up on their private lands the statue of Heracles sent by his own father, he dismissed them from the priesthood and confiscated to the crown the village in which the statues had been erected. MX II. 14, pp. 151-152.

Առաջին գործ զմեհեանսն շինել կամեցաւ: Իսկ քրմացն, որ եկեալ էին ի Յունաց, զմտաւ ածեալ, զի մի՛ ի խորագոյն Հայս վարիցին՝ պատճառեցան ըղձութիւնս, իբր թէ դիքն անդէն կամիցին զբնակիլն: Որում հաւանեալ Տիգրան, կանգնեաց զՈղիմպիական պատկերն Դիոսի յամուրն յԱնի, եւ զԱթենայն ի Թիլ, եւ զԱրտեմիդայ զմիւս պատկերն յԵրիզայ, եւ զԵփեստուն ի Բագայառինջ: Բայց զԱփրողիտեայ զպատկերն, իբրեւ Հերակլեայ տարփաւորի, առ նորին պատկերիդ Հերակլեայ հրամայեաց կանգնել յաշտից տեղիսն: Եւ ցասուցեալ ընդ Վահունիսն եթէ ընդէ՛ր յիւրեանց սեպհականին իշխեցին կանգնել զպատկերն Հերակլի, զառաքեալն ի նորին հօրէ՝ ընկեներ զնոսա ի քրմութենէն, եւ զգիւղն յարքունիս առնու, յորում պատկերքն կանգնեցան:

4.

He himself went down to Mesopotamia, and finding there the statue of Barshamin, he embellished it with ivory, crystal, and

[†] Eriza, according to Tommaséo, Langlois, etc. However, Eriza is the genitive-dative form of Ere'z. See the two instances in Agat'angeghos (Venice, 1862) pp. 49 and 590.

silver. He ordered that it should be brought and set up on the town of T'ordan. MX II. 14, p. 152.

գիշխանութիւն գօրուն. բայց միայն գթագական ասպետութիւնն ո՛չ հանէ։ Ինքն իջանէ ի Միջագետս, եւ գտեալ անդ զԲարշամինայ զպատկերն, գոր ի փղոսկր եւ ի բիւրեղէ կազմեալ էր արծաթով՝ հրամայէ տանել կանգնել յաւանին Թորդան։

From these passages cited above it follows that according to the chronology of Movses Xoranats'i, toward the beginning of the first century before our era, nine foreign idols were transported to the pagan temples of Armenia by order of the two conquering monarchs, Artashes and Tigran. Three of these statues came from Asia Minor, five from Greece, and one from Mesopotamia:

Found in Asia Minor

1. Artemis (I), whose statue was erected in Armavir.
2. Heracles, whose statue was erected in Ashtishat.
3. Apollo, whose statue was erected in Armavir.

Found in Greece

4. Dios, whose statue was erected in Ani.
5. Artemis (II), whose statue was erected in Erez.
6. Athena, whose statue was erected in T'il.
7. Hephestos, whose statue was erected in Bagayar'inj.
8. Aphrodite, whose statue was erected in Ashtishat.

Found in Mesopotamia

9. Barshame'n, whose statue was erected in T'ordan.

The city of Armavir which Artashes had designated as the recipient of the three statues taken from Asia Minor, but which only received the statues of Artemis and Apollo, was still

Armenia's capital. Artashes' grandfather Vagharshak already had placed there, along with statues of his ancestors, those of the Sun and the Moon (MX II. 8). When Eruand, Sanatruk's successor, abandoned Armavir and moved the court to the city of Ervandashat which he had built on the Arax not far from the Axurian River, he transported everything from the old capital to the new one, except for the idols. This suspicious monarch, fearful of having too many worshippers thronging in his vicinity, relocated the idols and statues to a town especially dedicated to the cult which he had built at a certain distance and named Bagaran (MX II. 39, 40). However Eruand's successor, Artashes II, in turn built a capital named after himself, Artashat. There he assembled everything which his predecessor had taken from Armavir and had used to adorn Eruandashat and Bagaran, also moving "the image/statue of Artemis and all of his patrimonial idols." Artashes also moved the statue of Apollo which was erected, however, "outside the city, close to the road" (MX II. 49). But the rest of the ancient idols of Armavir were not fated to join them there. When the first Sasanian king Artashir had the Armenian king Xosrov assassinated and conquered his kingdom, he destroyed the statues of the Sun and the Moon as well as those of Vagharshak's ancestors at Artashat (MX II. 77). Consequently only the statues of Artemis and Apollo were in the capital.

There is no evidence that any of the other statues had been moved. We need only replace the name of Armavir with that of Artashat to get a list of the eight sanctuaries. Two were at Artashat (those of Artemis and Apollo); one was at Ashtishat, with two idols side by side (Heracles and his lover, Aphrodite); and one in each of these locations: Ani, Erez, T'il, Bagayarindj, and T'ordan.

These sanctuaries were most irregularly spread throughout the Armenian territories (See figure 1: Map) Artashat was situated in central Armenia (valley of the Araxes), Ashtishat in southern Armenia (district of Taron); the five others were grouped into a narrow region of Upper Armenia formed by the three neighboring districts of Daranali, Ekegheats' (Akilisene), and Derjan (Derxene). The opposition of the Greek priests to the dispersion of their idols in the different provinces of Armenia only partly explains this peculiar state of affairs.

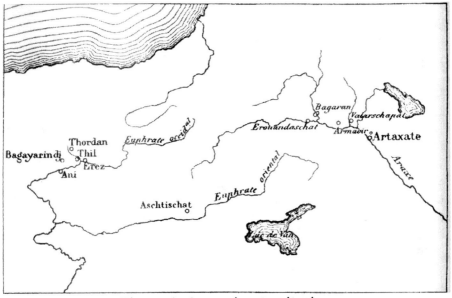

Figure 1: Armenian territories

II

Toward the end of the 3rd century A.D. and the beginning of the 4th century—the date is uncertain—about four hundred years after the diffusion of Greek idols into the temples of Armenia, King Tiridates (Trdat) resided at Vagharshapat, not far from the modern city of Erevan. As a result of quite extraordinary events which are narrated in the marvelous book of Agat'angeghos, and thanks to the preaching of Gregory the Illuminator, Tiridates embraced the Christian faith. Even before being baptized he "spontaneously" commanded that the ancient national gods "who are not gods" should be removed from the soil of Armenia and that even their memory should be effaced.

139

So commenced a true war whose most salient points we will review here. Trdat was accompanied by his nobles and soldiers; they were needed to fight against armed demons who frequently defended access to the pagan temples. He also took along Gregory and, leaving his residence at Vagharshapat headed first to Artashat to destroy the altars of the goddess Anahit. However, before entering that city he found "on the road" the sanctuary of the god Tir (or Tiur), which he destroyed before destroying that of Anahit (Agat'. p. 584 ff.).

Thereafter saint Gregory began an evangelizing tour of the cities, towns, and villages of Armenia, marking the places for future churches, planting the cross, and teaching Christian doctrine (Agat'. p. 587 ff.).

War against the idols resumed. Trdat and saint Gregory headed for western Armenia where they found first the temple of the god Barshimnia in the village of T'ordan in the district of Daranaghi. The temple was destroyed and the statue of the god smashed to pieces. saint Gregory stopped in this district to convert the residents and to successfully pursue the demons (p. 588 ff.).

From there the king and the saint went to the fortress of Ani where the tombs of the Armenian kings were located, to destroy the altars of Aramazd, father of all the gods. In the neighboring district of Ekegheats', in the town of Erez, they destroyed the temple of Anahit. Then they crossed the Gayl (Lycus) River and demolished the temple of Nane, Aramazd's daughter, in the town of T'il. Finally with Gregory continuing to evangelize and Trdat to relate the miracles he had experienced, they arrived in the district of Derdjan and, in the town of Bagayar'inj, they razed the temple of the god Mher [Mithra], son of Aramazd (p. 590 ff.).

After destroying the sanctuaries of Upper Armenia, they took a break. The king and his court had converted to Christianity but still had not been "illuminated by baptism," for Gregory, not being a priest, could not confer it. Consequently, a great assembly was held at Vagharshapat which resolved to send him to Caesarea of Cappadocia to be ordained by the bishop there.

saint Gregory departed "in the royal chariot," escorted by many nobles and 10,000 soldiers. At Caesarea bishops Leontius and other bishops performed the laying on of hands and thus he received "authority in heaven and on earth and the keys to the kingdom of heaven." In conformity with the rites he became priest [and bishop] and head of the Church of Armenia. Then he returned to his country, honored everywhere he passed and bringing with him precious relics given to him by saint Levontius (p. 594 ff.).

When he reached the Armenian border, Saint Gregory learned that in the land of Taron a sanctuary had been spared and was still standing. This was the Vahevahean ‡ temple, sacred to the god Vahagn, the eighth § of the famous sanctuaries, the "place of sacrifice of the kings of Greater Armenia"; it was full of riches and was located in the town of Ashtishat. Agat'angeghos provides us with more details about this celebrated temple than on any of the others. Despite this, his description is not that clear. We see that the Vahevahean contained three altars or temple, the first dedicated to the god Vahagn, the second to the Golden Mother, and the third to the goddess Astghik, Vahagn's lover, whom the Greeks called Aphrodite **. As far as the second, the Golden Mother, this epithet refers to the goddess Anahit whom we have already encountered at Artashat and Erez. However, here the text does not provide her name.

The destruction of the Vahevahean was accompanied by extraordinary portents. The soldiers sent to destroy the temple, led astray by the demons, were unable to find the entrance.

---

‡ The word Vahe'vahe'an is still not sufficiently explained. It seems to stem from a form of Vahe'vahe', which is equivalent to Vahagn. Cf. Gelzer, *Zur armen. Goetterlehre.* p. 104; Hübschmann, *Armenische Grammatik*, I, pp. 76, 508.

§ *The eighth...* The majority of translators have not considered that the text here plainly concerns the *eighth* [and last] idol temple destroyed by saint Gregory. Tommaséo: *celebrato col nome d'ottavo culto del cosi detto Vaacno;* Langlois: *célèbre par le nom de la huitième statue du dieu appelé Vahak'n;* Hübschmann has translated it best: *das achte berhmte Heiligthum, Arm Gramm.* I, 76.

** The Armenian text, literally translated calls the third temple "the sleeping chamber *seneak* of Vahagn." The same word *seneak* also means "concubine."

Their iron tools could not mar the walls. When Saint Gregory observed this, he ascended a hill opposite the temple and called on the aid of the Almighty. From the cross he held in his hand "a strong wind" blew which went and leveled the building such that no "trace" of it remained there.

It was only after this that saint Gregory built the first church and began to baptize the Armenians. When King Trdat in his royal residence in Vagharshapat heard about the return of the bishop, he hastened to go before him and to receive baptism on the banks of the Euphrates River with his court and his entire army.

It is not our intention to consider the historical veracity of these remarkable passages which we have summarized here. We accept the facts as they are narrated to us and confirm that eight temples were destroyed, two as Artashat and one each in the towns of T'ordan, Ani, Ere'z, t'il, Bagayar'inj and Ashtishat, the latter having three idols, two of which are named.

III

It is perhaps unnecessary to observe that the place names cited here are identical with those mentioned previously in the passages from Movses Xorenats'i. Only the gods' names are different: where Agat'angeghos provides Armenian names, Movses gives Greek names [††]. This difference, which is very

---

[††] 1. In the rest of Movses Xorenats'i's *History* the names of the gods used by Agat'angeghos are seldom encountered. It further appears that that author displays a certain repugnance to regard them in these forms as Armenian deities. Aramazd, the most frequently cited (I. 31; II. 53, 86; III. 15) is never called a god in Armenia (II. 53), rather he is a god of the Iberians (II. 86). Vahagn (I. 31; II. 8, 12), though a son of an Armenian king has a statue among the Iberians who sacrifice to it (I. 31). Barschame'n (II. 14; I. 14 under the name Barscham) is worshipped by the Syrians. Mihr appears only once and as a Persian god (III. 17). Astghik also appears just once (I. 6) as a sister of Zrvan, Titan, and Yapetosthe' who are, according to Movses, Shem, Ham, and Japhet (see A. Carrière, *Moïse de Khoren et les généalogies patriarcles* ,

apparent at first completely disappears if we use the Greek ‡‡ rather than the Armenian text of Agat'angeghos, which translates the names exactly as we find in Movses. The table below clearly shows the similarities and dissimilarities of the three manuscripts.

AGATHANGE			MOISE DE KHOREN	
Sanctuaires.	Divinités.		Sanctuaires.	Divinités.
—	Texte arménien.	Texte grec.	—	—
Artaschat	Anahit	*Artémis*	Armavir ²	*Artémis*
			Aschtischat	*Héraclès*
Artaschat	Tir (ou Tiur)	*Apollon*	Armavir ²	*Apollon*
Thordan	Barschimnia	*Barsamènè*		
Ani	Aramazd	*Dios* ²	Ani	*Dios*
Érèz	Anahit	*Artémis*	Érèz	*Artémis*
Thil	Nauè	*Athéna*	Thil	*Athéna*
Bagayaridj	Mihr	*Héphestos*	Bagayarindj	*Héphestos*
	Vahagn	*Héraclès*		[*Héraclès*]
Aschtischat {	N	N	Aschtischat	. . . . . .
	Astlik	*Aphrodite*		*Aphrodite*
			Thordan	*Barschamèn*

The only difference is in the form of the names. Where the text of Movses Xorenats'i has Barshaminay, the regular genitive of

p. 42), thus she is Noah's daughter! Anahit, who was the great goddess of Armenia according to the unanimous testimony of antiquity, is never mentioned. Neither are the deities Tir and Nane'.

‡‡ *Agathangelus und die Akten Gregors von Armenien, neu herausgegeben von Paul de Lagarde* (Goettingen, 1887).

143

Barshame'n, the text of Agat'angeghos has the rather unusual form Barshimnia. It seems certain that the latter form is a copyist's error for Barshamina as the corresponding place in the Greek manuscript has Barshamenes. Such an error in a proper name will not surprise those who deal with Armenian manuscripts.

It is also noteworthy that this same word occupies different places in the two lists. While the sanctuary at T'ordan appears right after that of Artashat in Agat'angeghos, in Movses Xorenats'i it is in last place. We shall explain this later. However, for now let us leave "Barshame'n" to one side and examine the order of the other names in the table.

Since Movses Xorenats'i himself took the precaution of informing us that the idols of Artashat had been transported there from their previous home in Armawir (see I. above), and that the altar of Heracles which had been destined for Armawir was set up at Ashtishat, we may conclude that both the temples and the idols appear in the same order in Agat'angeghos and Movses Xorenats'i.

A resemblance of this nature cannot be regarded as simple coincidence. We must suppose some dependence between the two texts.

The following remarks support such a conclusion:

A. The name Barshame'n which is of Semitic origin, though certainly corrupted (perhaps for Belshamin) is not found anywhere else in Armenian literature.

B. The same expression "places of sacrifices (*yashtits' teghik*)" is used to give a folk etymology for the city of Ashtishat. However, the full expression "places of sacrifice of the kings of Greater Armenia" which is used in the text of Agat'angeghos (p. 606) regarding the Vahe'vahe'an temple is greatly abridged in the text of Movses Xorenats'i to "places of sacrifice" (p. 14) and employed as a proper noun in place of Ashtishat.

C. When Trdat went from Vagharshapat to Artashat to destroy

the sanctuary of Anahit-Artemis, before entering the city and "on the road" he encountered the temple of the god Tir-Apollos (Agat'. p. 584). Here the matter is about the road the king was traveling on, that is "the road which went [from Vagharshapat] to the city of Ashtishat," which Agat'angeghos had previously referred to (p. 151). Now when Movses Xorenats'i is relating how king Artashes II transported the idols at Bagaran to his new capital at Artashat (MX II. 49), he adds "but the king erected the statue of Apollo outside the city, close to the road." this last remark is rather imprecise, since there was more than one road leading to Artashat.

D. According to Movses Xorenats'i (p. 12) the statue of Dios was erected §§ "in the fortress of Ani (*yamurn yAni*)." The Armenian appears to be an abridgement of Agat'angeghos' (p. 590) more expansive expression "in the fortified place called Ani (*yamur tegin yanuaneal yAni*)." The word ordinarily used to designate the *fortress* of Ani is *amrots'* (MX II. 12, 38).

Now we come to the dissimilarities found in the study of the text of Agat'angeghos and Movses Xorenats'i. Let us try to clarify the three points already mentioned:

1. The place assigned to the god Barshame'n.

2. The change in the destination for Heracles' statue.

---

§§ Here we keep the genitive *dios* because all the other gods' names are in the genitive in the Greek text of agat'angeghos, as well as in the Armenian of Movses Xorenats'i. The passage concerning *dios* (ed. Lagarde, p. 67) presents a difficulty. the Armenian reads: "the altar of Aramazd, called the father of all the gods" whereas the Greek has "the altar of Cronos, father of *Dios* the supreme god." This would have contradicted the customary usage of the translator for whom Aramazd is always Zeus (see the word *Dia* in Lagarde's index). We have no doubt that this is a correction by a copyist who, not accepting Zeus as "the father of the gods" added the name of Cronos (Saturn). To Movses Xorenat'si, *Dios* is the nominative form, the genitive being *Diosi*. Moreover *Dios* is ordinarily employed as a nominative in Armenian. See the numerous examples in Father Dashean's booklet *Agat'angeghos ar' Ge'orgay asori episkopos [Agat'angeghos according to Bishop George the Syrian]*.

3. The Greek names of the divinities replacing the Armenian.

1. Movses was unable to find a Greek equivalent for the Semitic name Barshame'n. Nonetheless he acknowledged the origin of this mythological entity, since the name with minor alteration appears in his history of the Armenian heroes. Barsham was said to be a tyrant of the race of giants who oppressed the country's southern reaches. Aram marched against him, attacked and defeated him and put him to flight from Korduats' to Asorestan. Barsham himself was killed by Aram's soldiers, but as he was renowned for his exploits, he was deified and worshipped for a long time by the Syrians (MX I. 14). Such euhemerisms are not rare in Movses.

Consequently it is toward the south that we should look for his statue, not in Asia Minor or in Greece, the theater of Artashes' exploits. The discovery of the idol of Barshame'n was made by Artashes' son Tigran when he conquered Mesopotamia and Syria. This is why Agat'angeghos' "glitteringly white god" (Barshamnia) in the aforementioned list is moved into last place [by Movses Xorenats'i] but with a statue made of white materials "ivory, crystal, and silver." We have noted elsewhere*** his less than conscientious and arbitrary use of the sources.

2. In the text of Agat'angeghos we find no reference to the disobedience of the Vahunik' ††† or of their transporting to Ashtishat the statue of Heracles which had been intended for Artashat. Agat'angeghos knows nothing about the Vahunis. Movses Xorenats'i, in his turn, appears to be ignorant of the Vahe'vahe'an temple, although he does give the name of the Vahunik' to the priestly family whose members served in the sanctuary of Ashtishat. This family derived from Vahagn whom Movses made a son of the Armenian king Tigran I (MX I. 31). They were entrusted with service in the temple and invested with the priesthood by Vagharsh (MX II. 8). We see that they lost these privileges and their goods at the beginning of the reign of Tigran the Great (II. 14). From then on, Movses no longer mentions them. Although the family name appears in a

*** *La légende d'Abgar*, p. 385.
††† Or Vahnunik'. The most recent editions of Movses have Vahunik'.

146

list of lords found in the *Life of Saint Nerses* (p. 34), this is the only reference to them and it is rather late. Beyond this, the ancient priestly family has left no other trace in all of Armenian literature. The Vahunik' are surely a product of Movses Xorenats'i's imagination.

It seems to us that the statue of Heracles prior to being finally erected in the place mentioned in Agat'angeghos's account had been reunited with the statues first sent from Greece. This provided Movses an opportunity to discourse about the Vahuni's disobedience and the end of their religious authority. It is the same with the third shipment of statues from Hellas accompanied by Greek priests whose protests prevented the dispersion of the statues throughout Armenian territory. Thus he explains why Agat'angeghos' text places five of the eight statues in a small corner of Upper Armenia.

Much of this derives from Movses' imagination, but a few other passages also reveal his characteristic method. When he says that the statue of Heracles is the work of Scyllis and Dipoenos of Crete, he had before him a source, probably Syriac, which may be found some day. Pliny speaks of a statue of Heracles among the works of Scyllis and Dipoenos (Pliny, *Natural History*, xxxvi, 4) and the chronography of Cedrenus (I, 564, ed. Bonn) also mentions the two sculptors, perhaps using a source related to the one Movses used. The last part of the sentence is not unique to Movses' source, i.e., "they erected it iin Taro'n in their hereditary/own (*sep'hakan*) village of Ashtishat." Here is the language that Ghazar P'arpets'i uses when describing how the Mamikoneans took saint Sahak's body for burial in Ashtishat: "They took it to the district of Taro'n to their own hereditary village named Ashtishat" (Ghazar, p. 104, ed. 1873) ‡‡‡. It is immediately obvious that dependence [Xorenats'i's text has on Ghazar's]. The idea which has Tigran erecting Aphrodite's statue by the side of that of Heracles at the sanctuary in Ashtishat, thereby uniting the two lovers naturally arose from and was justified by the text of Agat'angeghos.

---

‡‡‡ *taran i gawar'n Taro'noy i bnik giwghn iwr[eants'] sep'hakan˙ yanuaneal Ashtishat*, cf. Koriwn, ed. 1833, p. 25, and Moïse Khor. III. 67.

3. We have already spoken above about the names of the idols—with the exception of the god Barshame'n—being presented by Movses Xorenats'i in their Greek forms, forms corresponding exactly to those in the Greek edition of Agat'angeghos. Had Movses been independently translating them he could never have achieved such perfect correspondence. Moreover, excepting the passages more or less concerning our idols, Movses never provides Greek names for them, except when he is copying from other sources. Dios and Apollo do not appear elsewhere in his book. Artemis and Aphrodite appear in only one other passage (MX III. 33) where he is following Malalas §§§. Hephestos appears twice in the same chapter (MX I. 7) following Eusebius' *Chronicle/Chronicon* (vol. I, p. 200); similarly Heracles appears twice in the same chapter (MX II. 8) also following the *Chronicle* (vol. I, p. 58 ff.). Athena constitutes the sole exception, appearing twice in a letter of the emperor Julian (MX III. 15).

If Movses Xorenats'i himself did not translate these names, there are only two conclusions to be drawn. Either he was familiar with the Greek text of Agat'angeghos directly or indirectly, which is not impossible, or else the Armenian text of Agat'angeghos which Xorenats'i had before him contained the names in both their Armenian and Greek form. We cannot reject out of hand the existence of a such a parallel text. The text of Agat'angeghos which we are familiar with also contains such phrases as "Astghik, who is Aphrodite," and in a passage in P'awstos Buzand describing the destruction of the sanctuary of Ashtishat—which clearly derives from Agat'angeghos—we read "Heracles, that is to say, Vahagn" (ed. 1889, p. 37). These may be traces of an old recension of the text of Agat'angeghos which is now lost.

These diverse observations which we have presented thus far accentuate further the nature of the relationship between the two documents. Moreover they indicate that Movses Xorenats'i's text is not the older one. The precedence of Agat'angeghos is evident in other ways. Without making observations which pertain to literary history, Agat'angeghos's text further

---

§§§ A. Carrière, *Nouvelles sources de Moïse de Khoren.* Supplément, p. 22.

148

demonstrates precedence in the order of the names, which simply follows the itinery of saint Gregory in his three campaigns about the idols:

1. From Vagharshapat to Artashat;

2. From Vagharshapat to Upper Armenia;

3. From Vagharshapat to Caesarea and a return via Ashtishat.

Movses observes the same order, but encountering a reference to a second temple of Anahit-Artemis, one in Artashat and the other in Ere'z, he is forced to have two statues of Artemis brought to Armenia, one from Asia Minor and the other from Greece. This circumstance alone is sufficient to demonstrate the artificial nature of his account.

We may regard it as proven that Movses Xorenats'i, in creating his list of the idols introduced into Armenia, was following the account of the destruction of the temples provided by Agat'angeghos.

IV

In the period in which Movses Xorenats'i lived one could form only an imperfect idea about the ancient religion of Armenia. The tradition had vanished. The books which circulated in great number then spoke very little about ancient faiths as well as about foreign faiths. The exception were some polemical works which countered Sasanian Mazdaism. The old sanctuaries had been consecrated to the new cult, and the old festivals had been Christianized. What happened in Armenia had happened in all countries which had converted to Christianity with the exception of Greece and Rome, where a brilliant and indestructible literature maintained at least the memory of the old worship.

It is not impossible that the account in Agat'angeghos about the destruction of the sanctuaries was the only text available from which Movses Xorenats'i could derive information about Armenia's national pagan faith, just as today it remains the only basis for all research on the Armenian pantheon. In any case, Movses was familiar with it and used it. That document provided him with a sort of official list of the old sanctuaries and the idols worshipped in them. He made extensive use of it ****, but did not introduce any of its information anywhere in his *History* in the chronologically appropriate places. For example when speaking of Trdat, he does not mention the gods he worshipped or anything about the destruction of the sanctuaries in the relevant passages. This is a noteworthy shortcoming of the section of Movses' book where he *must speak* of Armenia's conversion to Christianity.

Information drawn from Agat'angeghos' book was used, so to speak, regressively. Material was used to relate the origin and transplantation into Armenia of the idols destroyed by saint Gregory. Thus one could know the provenance of *each* of them. The idols were true trophies, marvelous booty which the Armenians had a right To be proud of, since they were simultaneously products and proofs of their kings' conquests in Asia Minor, Greece, and Mesopotamia. Perhaps Movses Xorenats'i also wanted thereby to assign a Greek origin to Armenian idolatry. Indeed he never says a word about the statues which were already standing in the sanctuaries and is more interested in how the idols at Ani were distributed to the neighboring towns. However this last issue is outside the scope of our present investigation.

If, as we believe we have established, the introduction of Greek idols into Armenia does not correspond to any actual event but is instead the product of Movses Xorenats'i's imagination, then the worth of many chapters of his book is gravely compromised.

**** One can get some idea of this from the following detail: according to Movses Xorenat'si the two statues at Artashat are 1. Artemis-Anahit, and 2. Apollo-Tir. However the sanctuaries were destroyed in reverse order, first that of Tir followed by that of Anahit. Nonethless Movses Xorenats'i reproduces the names in exactly the same order as they appear in the text of Agat'angeghos: "Trdat set out to destroy the temple of Anahit. *En route* he came upon the temple of Tir and destroyed it before that of Anahit" (Agat. p. 584).

Thus everything concerning the relocation of the statues from Armawir to Bagaran and from Bagaran to Artashat becomes nothing other than a development on the initial fiction. Moreover it reinforces the doubts which have arisen on many other points about the reigns of Eruand and Artashes II (Book II, 37-60). [As examples,] Artashes II had designated his son Mazhan as chief-priest of Aramazd at Ani (ch. 53) and sent an envoy to the temple at Ere'z to seek health and long life (ch. 60).

Events from these two reigns are narrated to us on the authority of another priest of Ani, Olympius (Ughiup), who purportedly had written a *History of the Temples* (*mehenakan patmut'iwnk*) (MX II. 48) [††††], but who is otherwise unknown. The god worshipped at Ani was Aramazd, that is for Movses Xorenats'i Jupiter *Olympian* which probably explains the priest's name. As for that "book," Movses never says that he held it in his hands, nor does he relate anything specifically deriving from it. He provides better information elsewhere (MX II. 66) where we read that the Syrian Bardesan "entered the fortress of Ani and read the *History of the Temples* [naturally the one by Olympius] where he also found information about the deeds of the kings. Bardesan, adding to it contemporary events, put the whole thing into Syriac and his work was subsequently translated into Greek" [‡‡‡‡]. Movses was

---

[††††] This is not the first time that Movses Xorenats'i tells us about the "temple histories which narrate the deeds of the kings." These "temple histories" existed in the archives at Edessa (II. 10) where they had been transported from Nisibis (II.27) and from the city of Sinope in Pontus (II. 38). In an earlier publication (*La légende d'Abgar*, p. 361 ff.) we have indicated that these alleged sources should be regarded as imaginary. Subsequently we have concluded that Movses took this idea of the "temple histories" from Eusebius' *Chronicle*, which he frequently used. [As Eusebius notes] Manetho wrote based on the histories of the temples (*i mehenakan patmut'eants'*) where the Greek text has *eichon anagraphas en tais irais biblois*; *ibid.* I, 133; see also I. 208.

[‡‡‡‡] This mention of a Syriac redaction and the translation from Syriac into Greek is taken from Eusebius (*History of the Church*, IV, 30; Arm. version p. 312) which is the source of much of Xorenats'i's chapter 66. However Eusebius' information about the writings of Bardesan has no mention of any "temple histories."

acquainted with the work of the Syrian heretic and gives and extract in this manner: "Bardesan says, according to the *History of the Temples* §§§§ that the last Tigran, king of Armenia, to honor the tomb of his brother the chief-priest Mazhan (II. 51, 53, 55) in the Town of altars (=Baguan) ***** in the district of Bagre'vand constructed an altar over the tomb where travelers could make sacrifices and find shelter for the night. In the same place subsequently Vagharsh instituted a solemn feast which was celebrated at the beginning of the New Year at the start of the month of Navasard."

It is impossible not to see in this feast, supposedly instituted by Vagharsh the one saint Gregory displaced with another one after Trdat's baptism in honor of the martyrs whose relics he had brought from Caesarea. It is true that the passage in Agat'angeghos (p. 623) presents difficulties in interpretation ††††. Some, such as Langlois find the god Amanor (*nor-tari*, "New Year") referenced here; others, such as Dulaurier, Gelzer, tec. find the god Vanatur ("shelter-giver"). Emin sees both Amanor and Vanatur, but equates these two deities. It must be conceded that the text in its present state, permits various interpretations. Movses Xorenats'i and the Greek translator of Agat'angeghos understood the passage in a different manner. Without a doubt they had before them a text somewhat different from ours. In any case, the citation from the *History of the Temples* by Bardesan derives from this passage in Agat'angeghos. To sum up, we see here a parallel to the introduction of the Greek statues into Armenia which highlights another instance of the way Movses Xorenats'i used the sources in a regressive manner.

---

§§§§ Reading *patmut'eants'* in place of the text's *pashtamants'*.
***** Baguan or Bagawan, "*awan* (village, small town) of the gods" (Hübschmann, *Arm. Gram.* p. 113). Agat (p. 612) states that this is a Parthian word and that its Armenian equivalent is *Dits'awan* ("town of idols/gods"). Movses Xorenats'i renders this as Bagnats'awan ("town of altars"), cf. II. 55; III. 67.
†††† Cf. H. Gelzer, *Zur armen. Götterlehre*, p. 132ff.

CPSIA information can be obtained at www.ICGtesting.com
Printed in the USA
LVOW131929120912

298551LV00018B/162/P

9 781604 441727